PIANO • VOCAL • GUITAR

ISBN 978-1-4584-2349-8

7777 W. BLUEMOUND RD. P.O. BOX 13819 MILWAUKEE, WI 53213

Visit Hal Leonard Online at
www.halleonard.com

CONTENTS

ALL CREATURES

Words and Music by
DAVID CROWDER

Moderately

D

mf

Bm7

G(add2)

D

All crea - tures of our God and
Thou rush - ing wind that art so
Let all things their Cre - a - tor

Bm7

King, lift up your voice and with us sing, O ______
strong, ye clouds that sail in heav'n a - long, O ______
bless, and wor - ship Him in hum - ble - ness. O ______

G(add2)
D
praise _ Him, Al - le - lu - ia! Thou burn - ing sun with gold - en
praise _ Him, Al - le - lu - ia! Thou ris - ing morn, in praise re -
praise _ Him, Al - le - lu - ia! Praise, praise the Fa - ther, praise the
Bm7
beam, thou sil - ver moon with soft - er gleam,
joice, ye lights of eve - ning, find a voice. O _
Son, and praise the Spir - it, Three in One.
G(add2)
D/F♯
G(add2)
praise _ Him, O _ praise _ Him, Al - le - lu - ia! Al - le -
To Coda
D/F♯
Asus
1
D
lu - ia! Al - le - lu - ia!

2
D
ia!
Bm7
G(add2)
D.S. al Coda
CODA
D
ia!
Praise, praise the Fa - ther, praise the

Bm7
Son, and praise the Spir - it, Three in One. O
G(add2)
D/F♯
G(add2)
praise Him, O praise Him, Al - le - lu - ia! Al - le -
D/F♯
Asus
G
lu - ia! Al - le - lu - ia!
A
Bm
A/C♯
Yeah, yeah, yeah, yeah. La di da la di da da. O al - le -

G
A
Bm
lu - ia! Al - le - lu - ia! O al - le - lu - ia! Al - le -
1
A/C♯
2
A/C♯
G
lu - ia! O al - le - lu - ia! Al - le - lu - ia! O al - le -
A
Bm
A/C♯
lu - ia! Al - le - lu - ia! O al - le - lu - ia! Al - le -
G
lu - ia!

AMAZING GRACE
(My Chains Are Gone)

Words by JOHN NEWTON
Traditional American Melody
Additional Words and Music by CHRIS TOMLIN
and LOUIE GIGLIO

G
C(add2)/G
G
grace that taught my heart to fear, and grace my fears re -
Lord has prom - ised good to me, His Word my hope se -
D/G
G
G(add2)/B
C(add2)
G
lieved. How pre - cious did that grace ap - pear the
cures. He will my shield and por - tion be as
D/G
G
C/G
G
C
hour I first be - lieved.
long as life en - dures.
My chains are gone, I've been set
mf
G/B
C
free. My God, my Sav - ior has ran - somed

D/G
G
Gsus2/B
Csus2
3fr
G
shine. But _ God, who _ called ___ me here be - low will

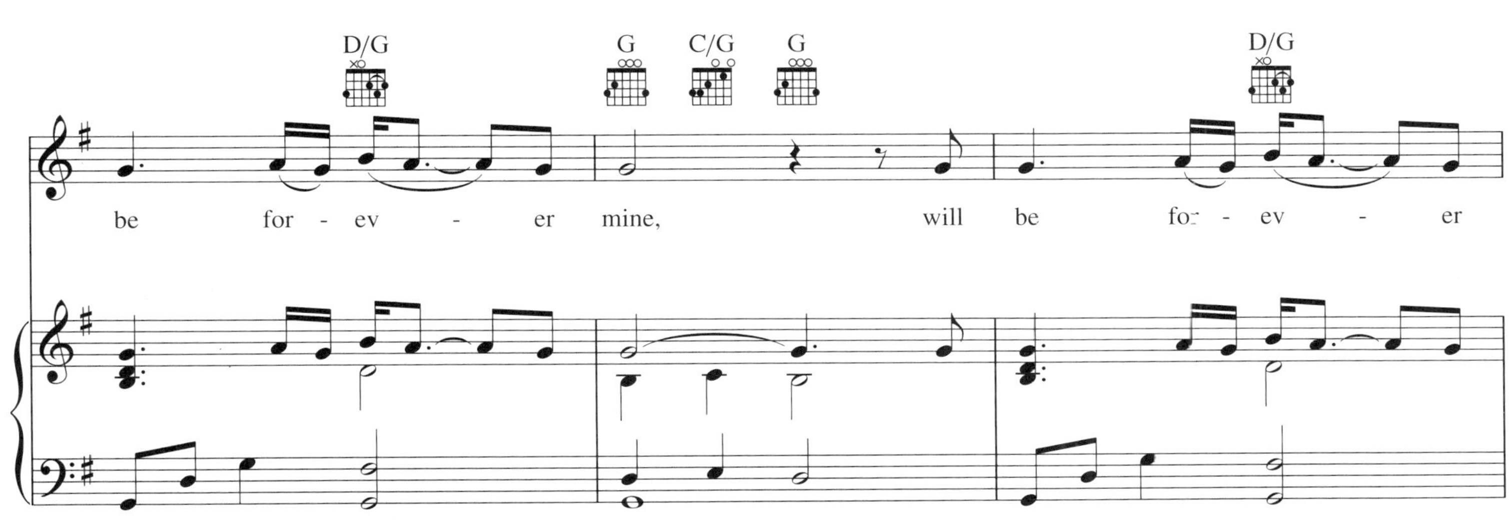
D/G
G
C/G
G
D/G
be for - ev - er mine, will be for - ev - er

G
C/G
G
D/G
G
mine. You are for - ev - er mine.
rit.

ALL THE WAY MY SAVIOR LEADS ME

Traditional Hymn
Arrangement and Additional Lyrics by
CHRIS TOMLIN and MATT REDMAN

B♭m7
A♭
E♭
who through life has been my guide?
A♭
D♭/A♭
All the way my Sav - ior leads me
A♭
D♭/A♭
and cheers each wind - ing path I tread.
B♭m7
A♭
E♭
Gives me grace for ev - 'ry tri - al,

B♭m7
A♭
4fr
E♭
3fr
feeds me with the liv - ing bread. You
D♭
A♭/C
E♭
3fr
lead me and keep me from fall - ing. You
D♭
A♭/C
E♭
3fr
car - ry me close to Your heart. And
B♭m7
A♭
4fr
E♭
3fr
sure - ly Your good - ness and mer - cy will

B♭m7
A♭
E♭sus
fol - low me.
A♭
D♭/A♭
All the way my Sav - ior leads me;
A♭
D♭/A♭
oh, the full - ness of His love.
B♭m7
A♭
E♭
Oh, the sure - ness of His prom - ise

B♭m7
A♭
E♭
in the tri - umph of His blood.
A♭
D♭/A♭
And when my spir - it, clothed im - mor - tal,
Fm7
E♭
D♭
wings its flight to realms of day,
B♭m7
A♭
E♭
E♭sus
E♭
this my song through end - less ag - es:

B♭m7
A♭
4fr
E♭
3fr
Je - sus led me all the way.
D♭
E♭
3fr
Je - sus led me all the way.
You
gradual cresc.
D♭
A♭/C
E♭
3fr
lead me and keep me from fall - ing.
You
mf
D♭
A♭/C
E♭
3fr
car - ry me close to Your heart.
And

B♭m7
A♭
4fr
E♭
3fr
sure - ly Your good - ness and mer - cy will
B♭m7
A♭
4fr
1
E♭sus
6fr
E♭
3fr
fol - low me. You
2
E♭sus
6fr
E♭
3fr
B♭m7
A♭
4fr
me, will fol - low
E♭sus
6fr
A♭
4fr
me.
dim.
mp

D♭(add2)/A♭
A♭
4fr
All the way my Sav - ior
D♭(add2)/A♭
A♭
4fr
leads me.
D♭(add2)/A♭
A♭
4fr
All the way my Sav - ior
D♭(add2)/A♭
A♭
4fr
D♭(add2)/A♭
leads me.

ANCIENT WORDS

Words and Music by
LYNN DeSHAZO

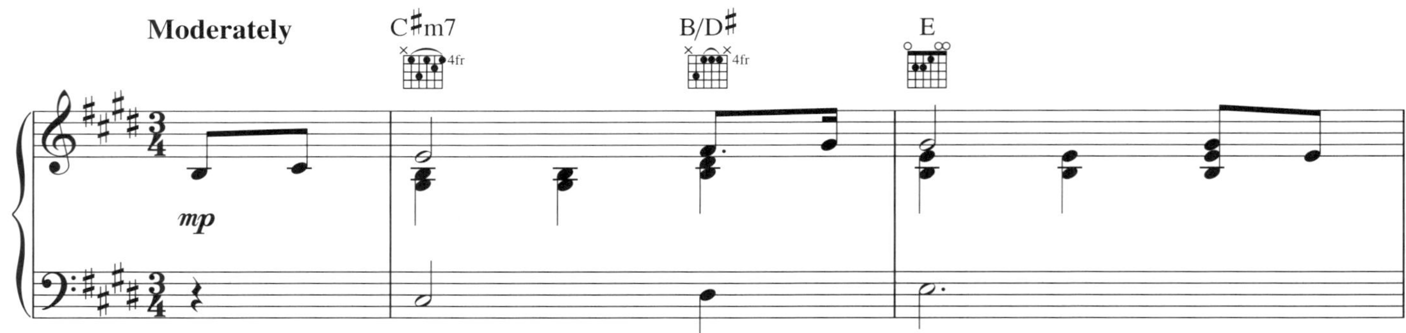

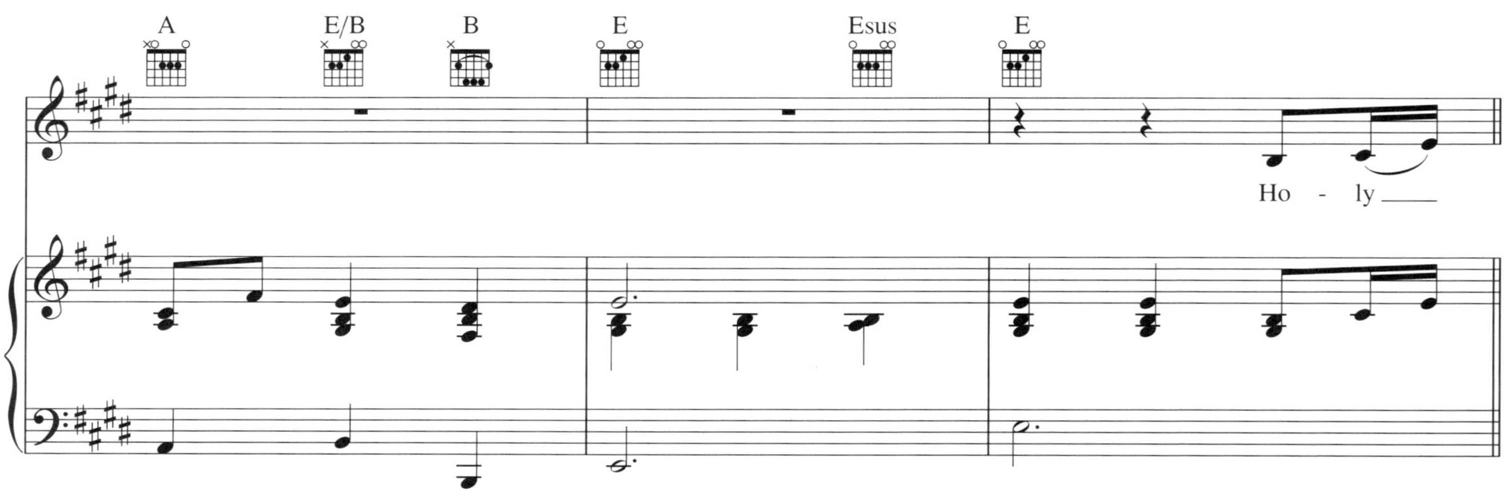

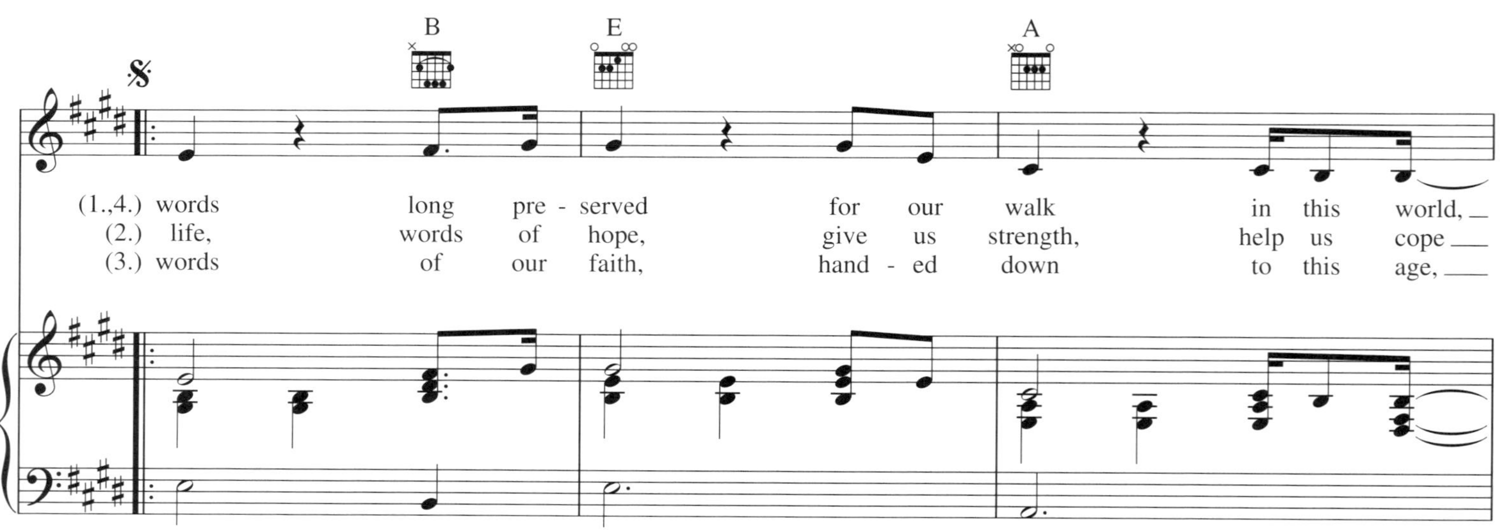

B
C♯m
B/D♯
E
E/G♯
4fr
they re - sound with God's own heart. Oh, let the
in this world wher - e'er we roam, an - cient
came to us through sac - ri - fice. Oh, heed the
A
E/B
B
E
Esus
1, 3
E
an - cient words im - part.
words will guide us home.
faith - ful words of Christ.
(2.) Words of
(4.) Ho - ly
2, 4
E
E/G♯
B
An - cient words, ev - er true, chang - ing
mf
F♯m7
E/G♯
A
B
C♯m
B/D♯
me and chang - ing you. We have come with o - pen

To Coda
E
A
E/B
B
E
B/D♯
4fr
hearts, oh, let the an - cient words im - part.
E
A
E/B
B
E
Esus
mp
E
D.S. al Coda
(with repeat)
(3.) Ho - ly
CODA
E
E/G♯
part. An - cient words, ev - er
f
B
F♯m7
E/G♯
A
B
true, chang - ing me and chang - ing you. We have

C♯m
B/D♯
E
A
E/B
B
come with o - pen hearts, oh, let the an - cient words im -
E
B/D♯
C♯m
B/D♯
part. We have come with o - pen
dim.
mp
E
A
E/B
B
C♯m7
hearts, oh, let the an - cient words im - part.
E/B
A
E/B
B
E
Oh, let the an - cient words im - part.
rit.

BEFORE THE THRONE OF GOD ABOVE

Words and Music by VIKKI COOK
and CHARITIE BANCROFT

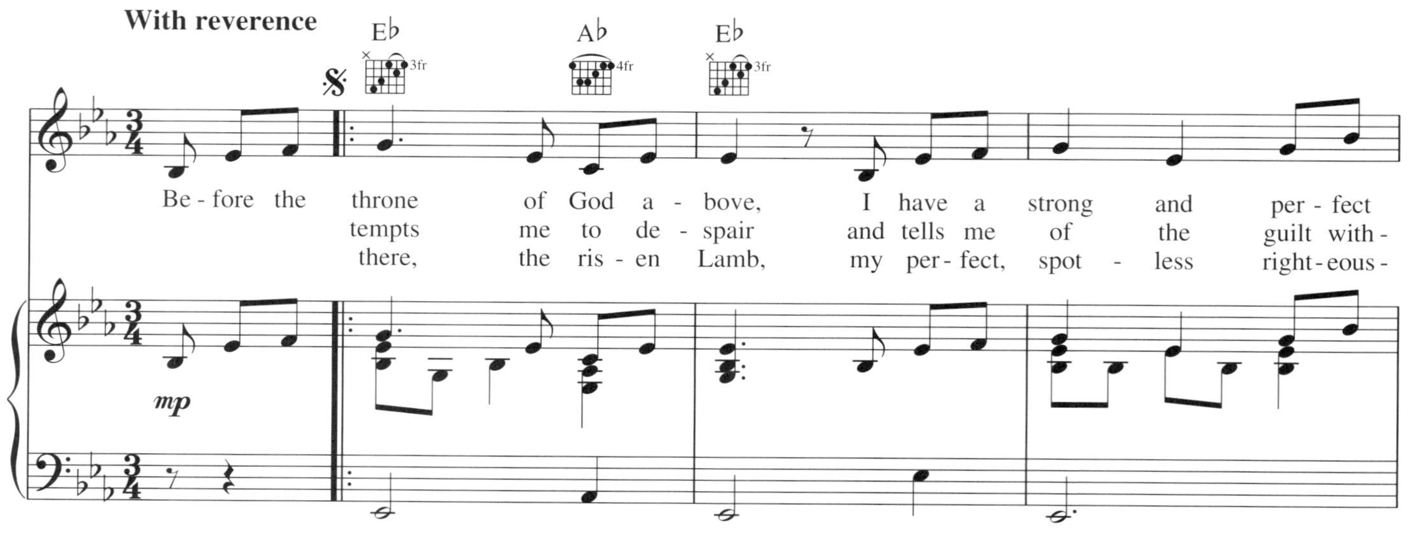

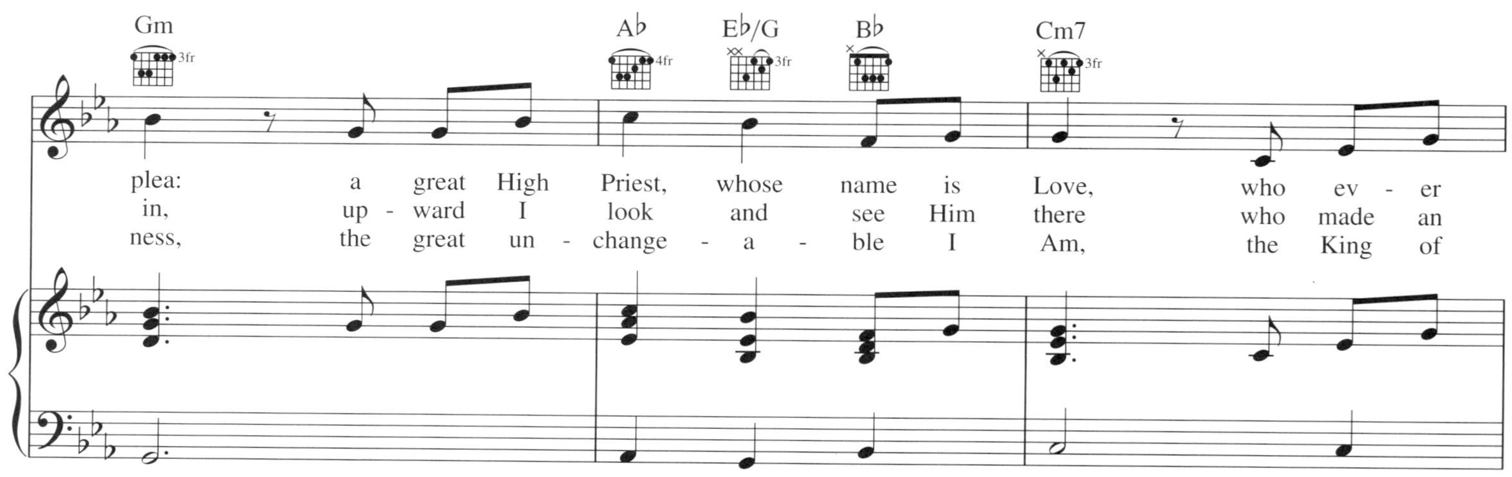

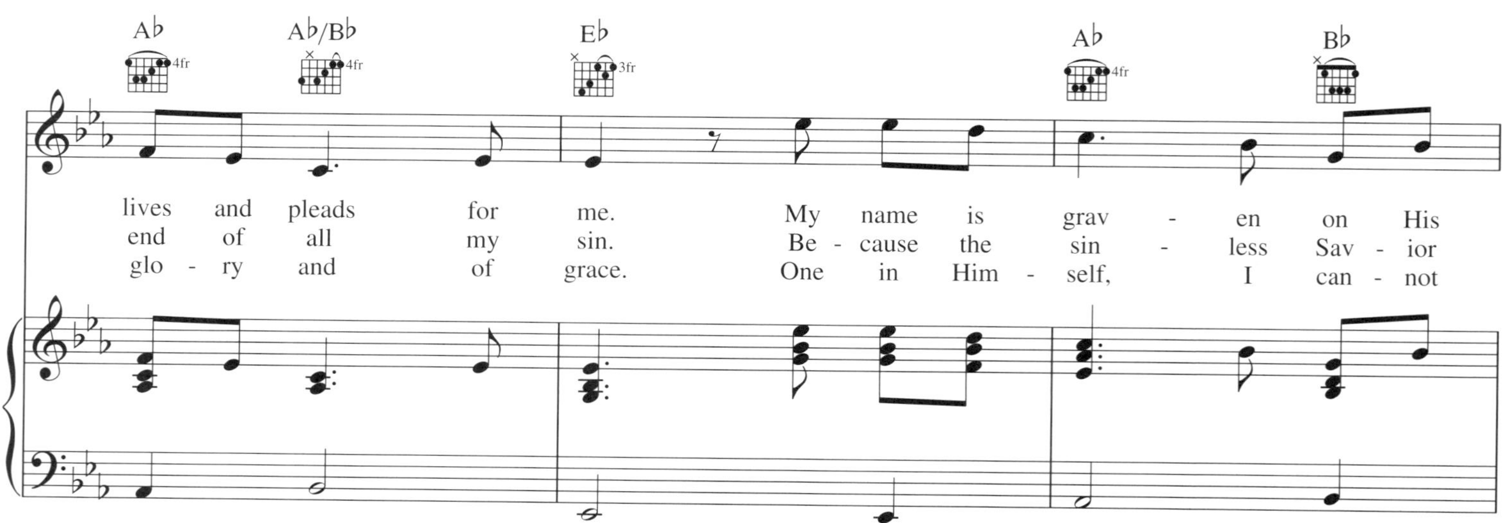

To Coda
E♭ A♭ B♭ Cm7
hands, my name is writ - ten on His heart. I know that
died, my sin - ful soul is count - ed free, for God the
die, my soul is pur - chased by His
A♭ B♭ Cm7 A♭ A♭/B♭
while in heav'n He stands, no tongue can bid me thence de -
Just is sat - is - fied to look on Him and par - don
Cm7 A♭ A♭/B♭
1
E♭
part, no tongue can bid me thence de - part. When Sa - tan
me, to look on Him and par - don
2
E♭ B♭
me. Al - le - lu -

E♭/G
Cm7
ia, al - le - lu - ia. Praise the
A♭
A♭/B♭
B♭
E♭
B♭/E♭
E♭
D.S. al Coda
One, ris - en Son of God. Be - hold Him
CODA
Cm7
A♭
B♭
Cm7
blood. My life is hid with Christ on high, with Christ my
A♭
A♭/B♭
Cm7
A♭
A♭/B♭
Sav - ior and my God, with Christ my Sav - ior and my

E♭
B♭
God. Al - le - lu - ia, al - le -
E♭/G
Cm7
A♭
lu - ia. Praise the One, ris - en
A♭/B♭
B♭
E♭
B♭/E♭
E♭
Son of God. Al - le -
B♭
E♭/G
lu - ia, al - le - lu -

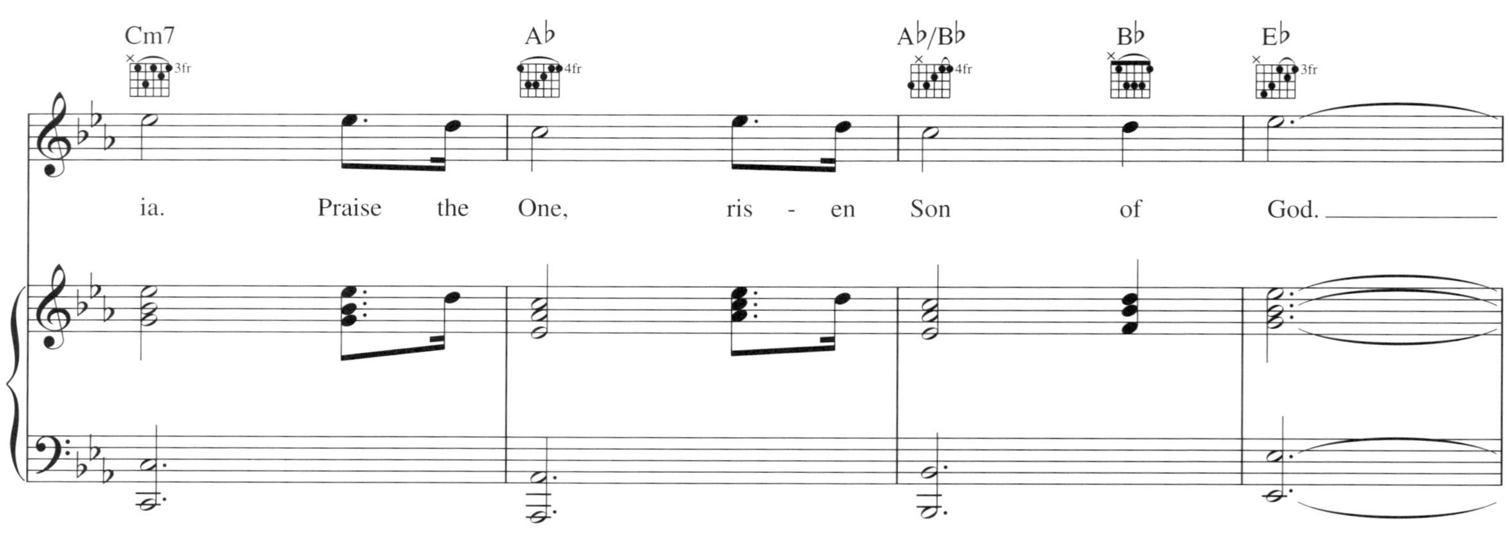
Cm7
3fr
A♭
4fr
A♭/B♭
4fr
B♭
E♭
3fr
ia. Praise the One, ris - en Son of God.

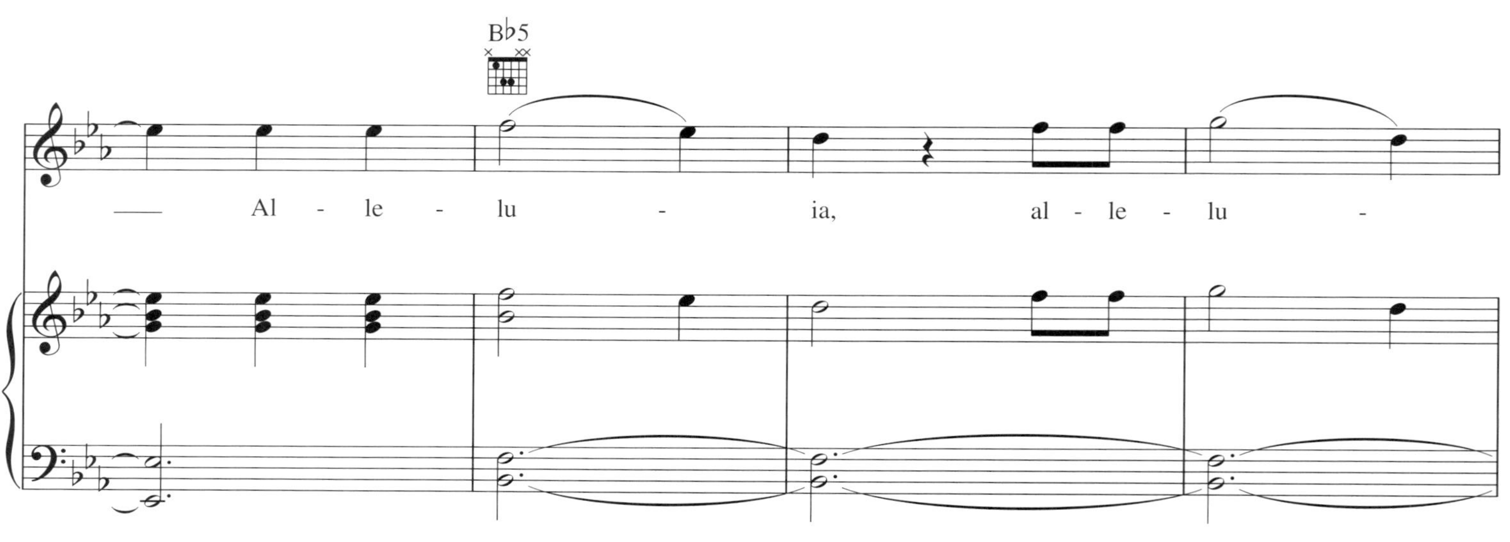
B♭5
Al - le - lu - ia, al - le - lu -

N.C.
ia. Praise the One, ris - en Son of God.

COME THOU FOUNT, COME THOU KING

Traditional
Additional Words and Music by
THOMAS MILLER

D
praise. Teach me some mel - o - dious son - net sung by
free. Now my soul can sing a new song, now my
Thee. Prone to wan - der, Lord, I feel it, prone to
flam - ing tongues a - bove. Praise the mount, I'm fixed up -
heart has found a home. Now Your grace is al - ways
leave the God I love. Here's my heart, Lord, take and
A/D
To Coda
1
G/B
A/C♯
D
on it, mount of Thy re - deem - ing love.
with me, and I'll
seal it, seal it
Dsus
D
Dsus2
D
I was

2
G/B
A/C♯
D
nev - er be a - lone.
Come Thou
G
D/F♯
G
Fount, come Thou King, come Thou pre - cious Prince of
D/F♯
Bm
D/F♯
G(add2)
Peace. Hear Your bride, to You we sing: Come Thou
1
2
D/A
A
D
D
A5/E
Fount of all bless - ing. Come Thou ing.

D.S. al Coda
D/F♯
A5/E
D/F♯
Gsus2
D/F♯
A5/E
D
Dsus2
O to
CODA
G/B
A/C♯
D
Dsus2
D
Dsus2
D
for Thy courts a - bove.
Vocal ad lib. on repeats
Dsus
D
Dsus2
1–3
D
4
D
Come Thou
G
D/F♯
G
Fount, come Thou King, come Thou pre - cious Prince of

D/F♯
Bm
D/F♯
G(add2)
Peace. Hear Your bride, to You we sing: Come Thou
D/A
A
1
D
2
D
A5/E
Fount of all bless - ing. Come Thou
ing.
D/F♯
A5/E
D/F♯
Gsus2
D/F♯
A5/E
D
D/F♯
A5/E
D
A5/E
D/F♯
A5/E
D/F♯
Gsus2
D/F♯
A5/E
D5
5fr

DOXOLOGY

Traditional
Additional Chorus and Arrangement by
DAVID CROWDER

E
flow. Praise Him, all crea - tures here be - low. Praise
A
D
Him a - bove, ye heav'n - ly hosts. Praise Fa - ther, Son and
A/E
E
A
Dsus2
A/C♯
Ho - ly Ghost. A - men!
Dsus2
A/C♯
Dsus2
A - men! A - men!

A/C♯
Dsus2
A/C♯
A - men!
Dsus2
E
A
E
mf
Praise God, from whom all bless - ings
A
E
flow. Praise Him, all crea - tures here be - low. Praise
A
To Coda
Him a - bove, ye heav'n - ly hosts. Praise

Dsus2
A/E
E
A
Fa - ther, Son and Ho - ly Ghost.
Dsus2
A/C♯
Dsus2
A/C♯
A - men!
A - men!
Dsus2
A/C♯
Dsus2
A - men!
A - men!
A/C♯
Dsus2
E
D.S. al Coda
Praise

CODA
A/E
E
A
Fa - ther, Son and Ho - ly Ghost.
Dsus2
A/C♯
Dsus2
A - men!
A - men!
mp
A/C♯
Dsus2
Join the an - gels now.
A - men!
A/C♯
Dsus2
A/C♯
So be it, Lord.
A - men!
It's true, it's true!

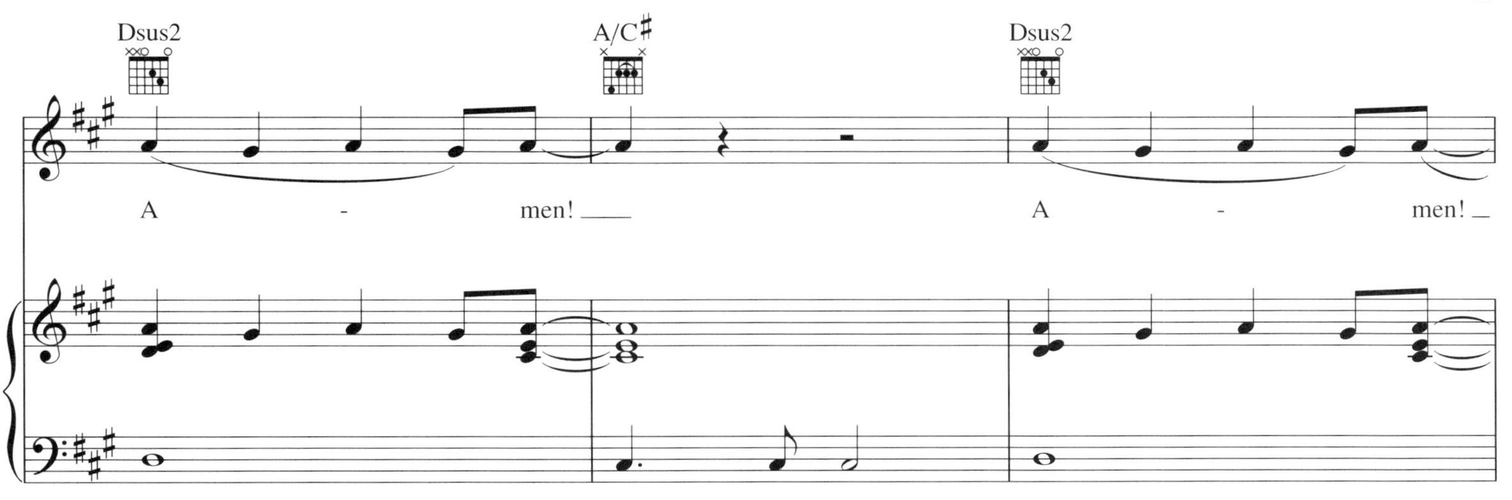
Dsus2
A/C♯
Dsus2
A - men!
A - men!

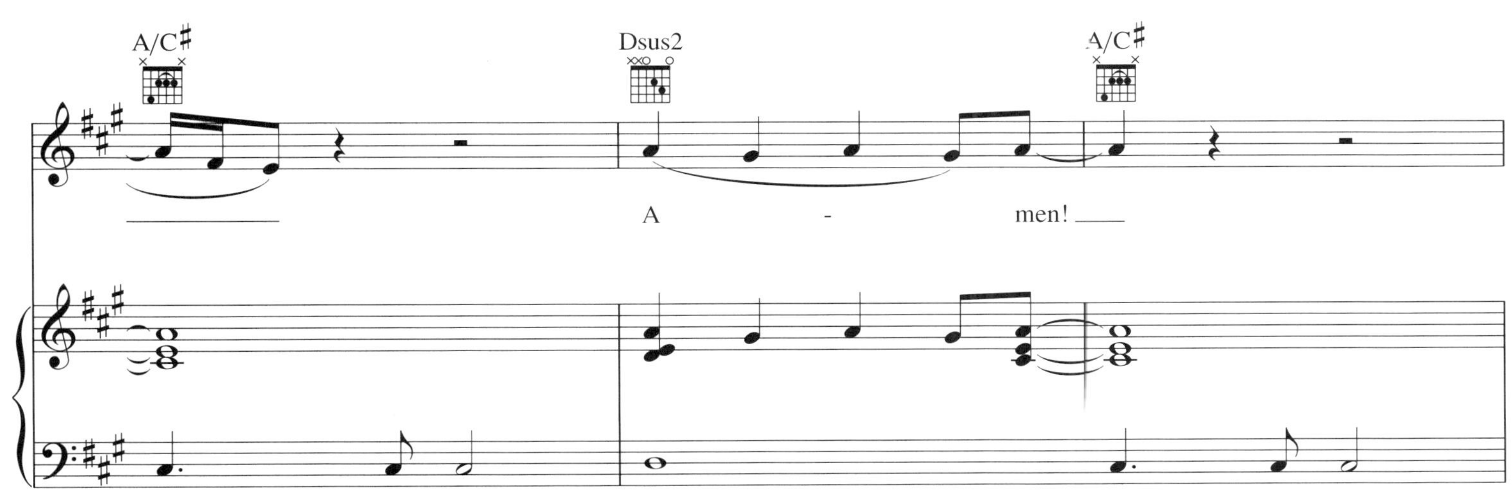
A/C♯
Dsus2
A/C♯
A - men!

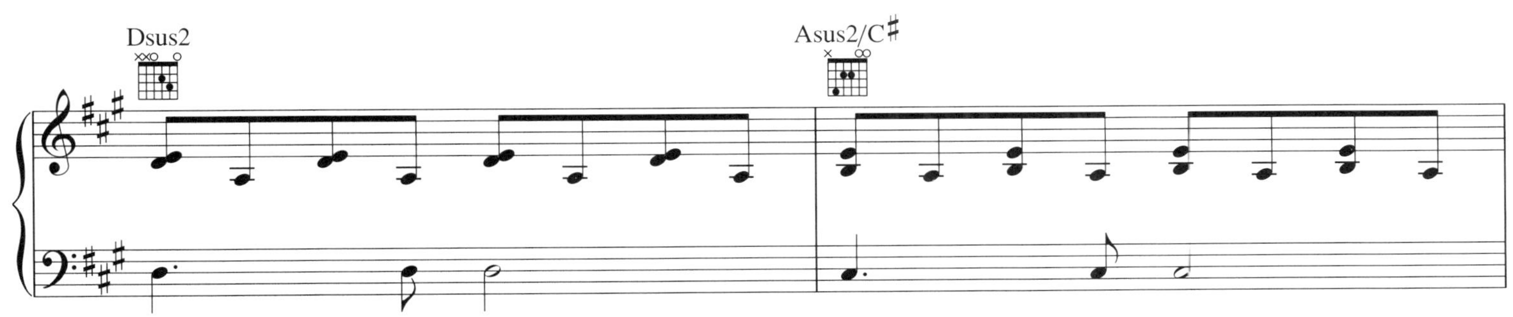
Dsus2
Asus2/C♯

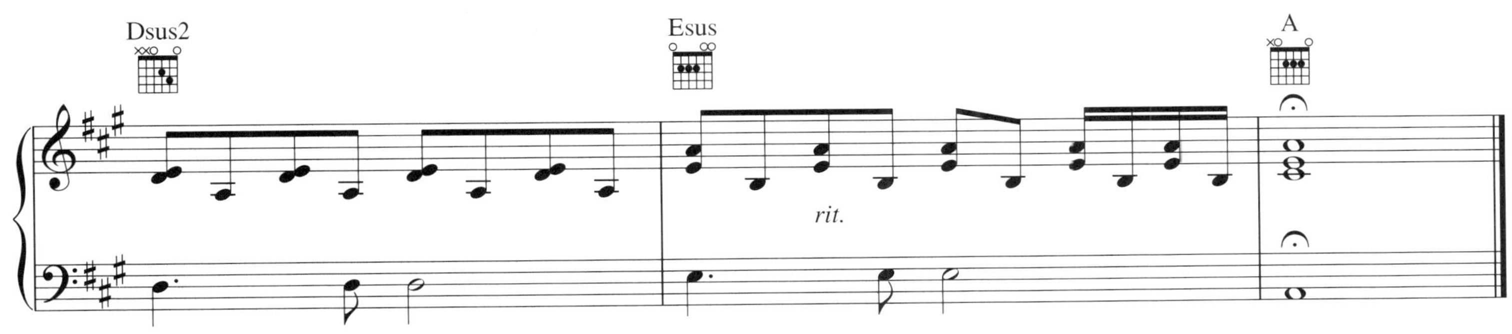
Dsus2
Esus
A
rit.

FAIREST

Words and Music by
GLENN PACKIAM

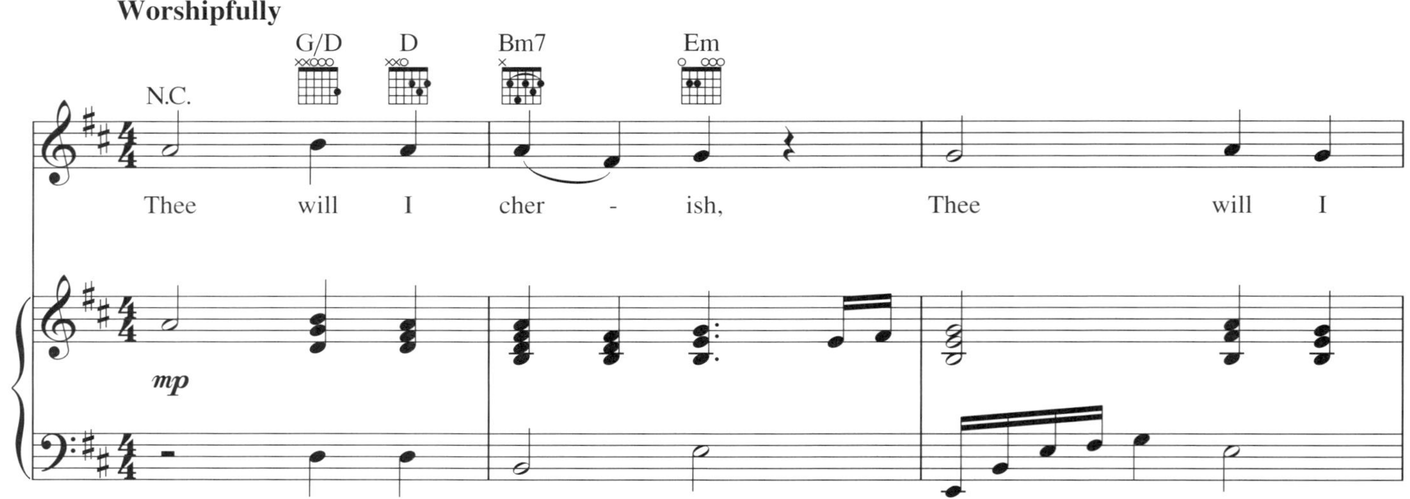

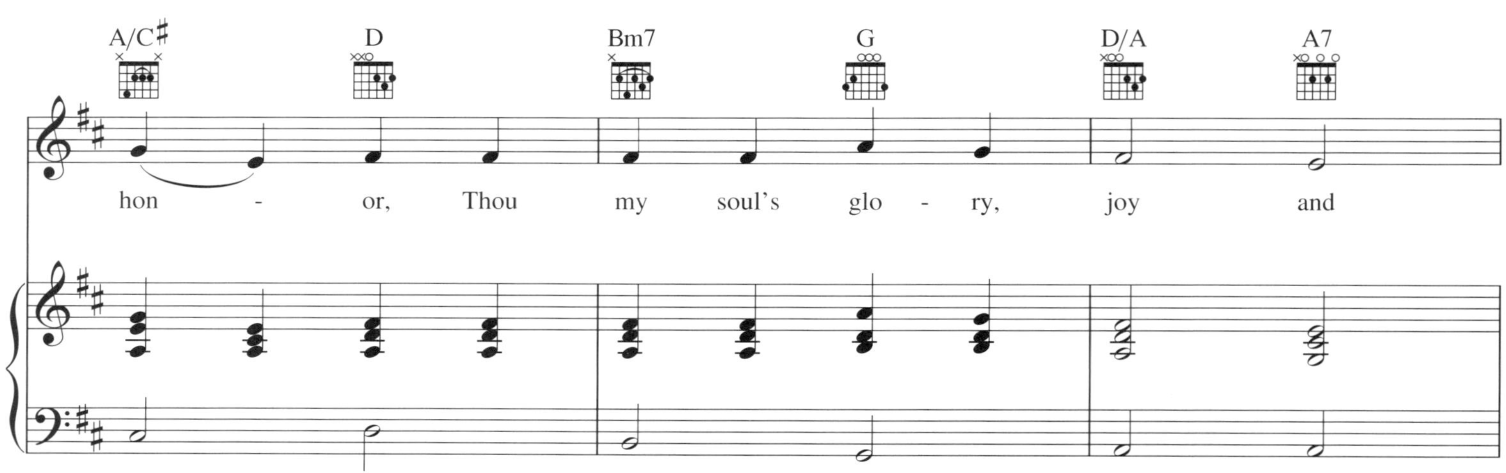

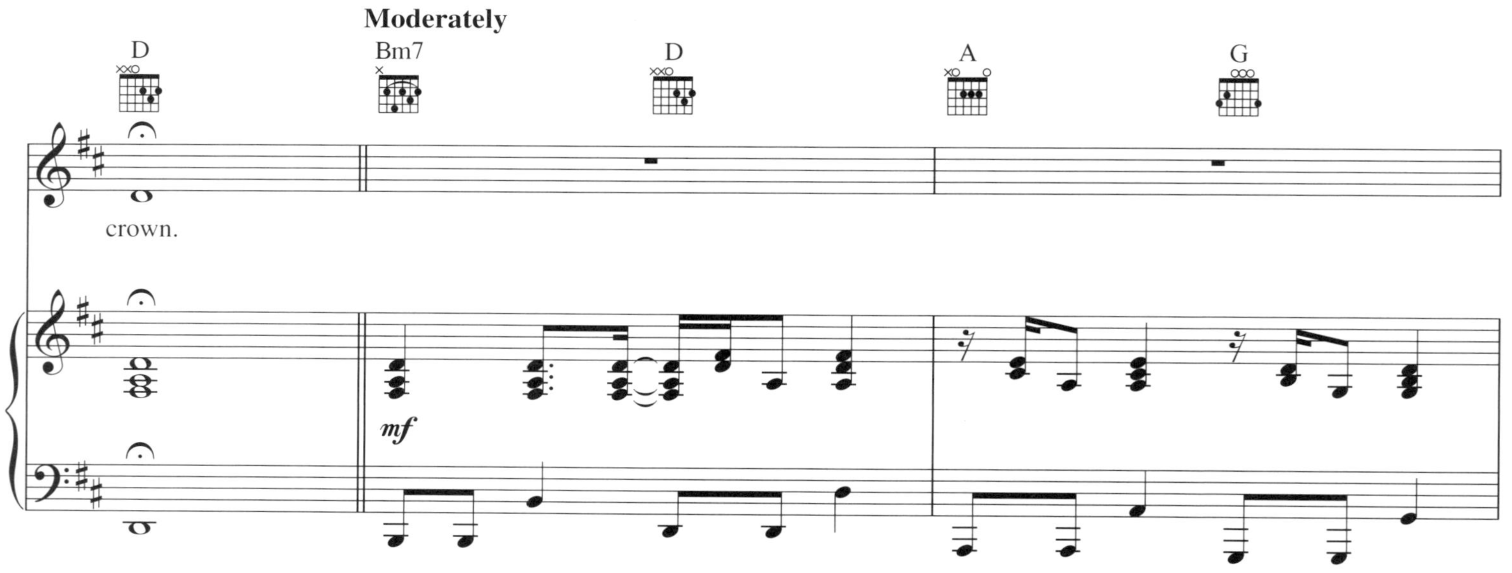

Bm7
D
A
Bm7
D
A
G
Bm7
D
A
Bm7
D
A
G
Bm7
D
Fair - est Lord Je - sus, Rul - er of all
Fair are the mead - ows, fair - er still the
Fair is the sun - shine, fair - er still the
A
D
Bm7
G
D/A
na - ture, O Thou of God and
wood - lands, robed in the bloom - ing
moon - light, and all the twin - kling

G/B Bm7 A/C♯ A D G/D D
man the Son. Thee will I
garb of spring. Je - sus is
star - ry host. Je - sus shines
Bm7 G/B Em7 A/C♯ D
cher - ish, Thee will I hon - or, Thou
fair - er, Je - sus is pur - er, who
bright - er, Je - sus shines pur - er than
Bm7 D G/D D/A A
1
Bm7 D
my soul's glo - ry, joy and crown.
makes the woe - ful heart to
all the an - gels heav'n can
A G Bm7 D A

2, 3
D
sing.
boast.
You are
A
Bm7
G
fair - er than the fair - est of ten thou - sand,
A
Bm7
G
love - li - er than all I've ev - er seen.
You are
A
Bm7
G
bright - er than the bright - est star in heav - en.

D/F♯
G
A
To Coda
Je - sus, You're ev - 'ry - thing to me.
D/F♯
G
A
D.S. al Coda
(take 2nd ending)
Je - sus, You're ev - 'ry - thing to me.
CODA
D/F♯
G
A
Je - sus, You're ev - 'ry - thing to me. You are
Bm7
G
fair - er than the fair - est of ten thou - sand,

A
Bm7
G
love - li - er ___ than all ___ I've ev - er seen. You are
A
Bm7
G
bright - er than ___ the bright - est star in heav - en.
D/F♯
G
A
Je - sus, ___ You're ev - 'ry - thing ___ to me. ___
D/F♯
G
A
Je - sus, ___ You're ev - 'ry - thing ___ to me. ___

Bm7
D
A
G
Bm7
D
A
D
Beau - ti - ful Sav - ior! Lord of all na - tions,
Bm7
G
D/A
G/B
Bm7
A/C♯
A
Son of God and Son of Man.
Slower
D
G/D
D
Bm7
G/B
Em7
Glo - ry and hon - or, praise, ad - o -
A/C♯
D
Bm7
D
G/D
D/A
A7
D
ra - tion, now and for - ev - er - more be Thine.

IN CHRIST ALONE

Words and Music by KEITH GETTY
and STUART TOWNEND

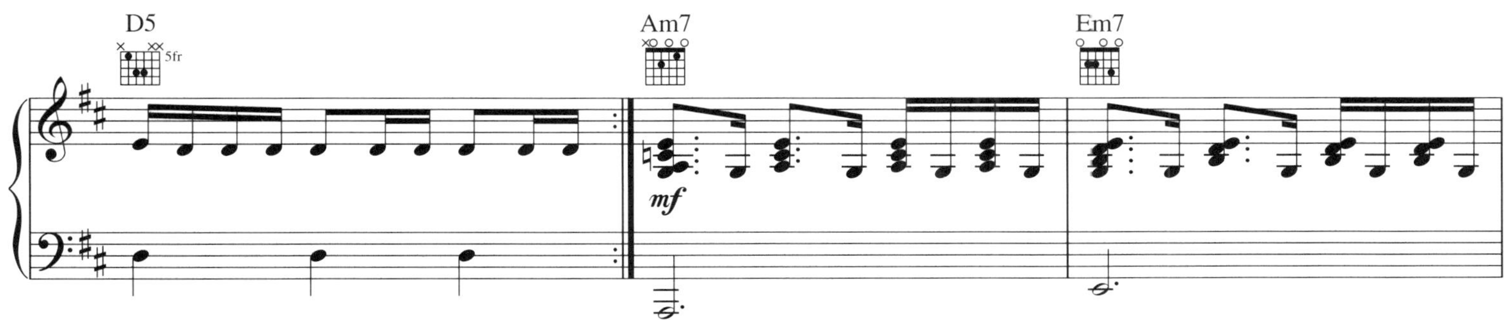

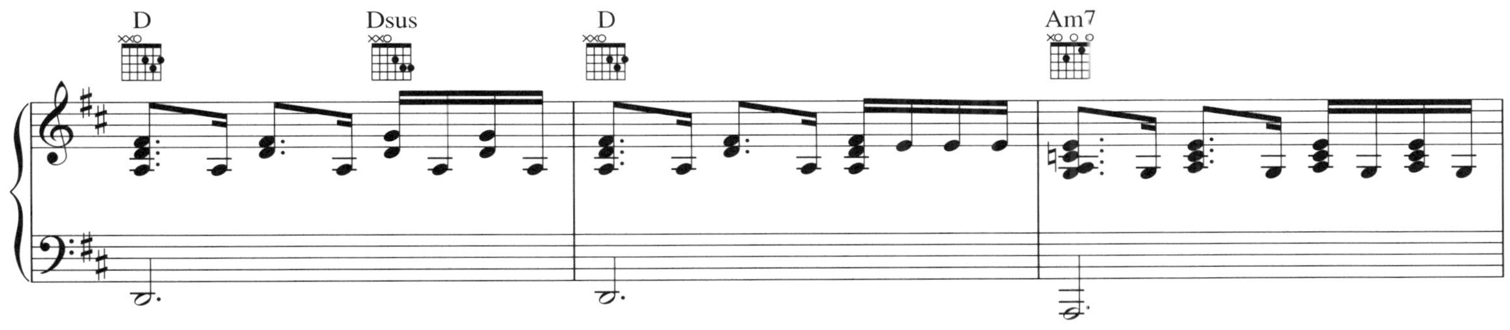

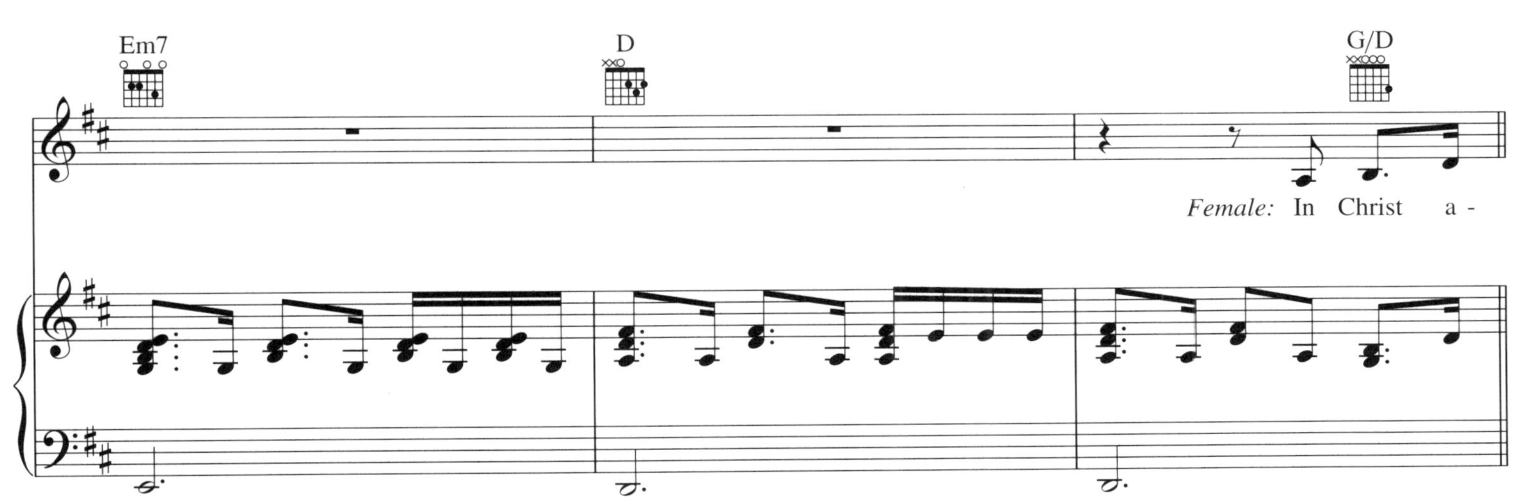

D A D/F♯ G D/F♯ Em G/A
3fr
lone my hope is found; He is my light, my strength, my
lone, who took on flesh, full - ness of God in help - less
D G D G A D/F♯
song. This cor - ner - stone, this sol - id ground, firm through the
Babe! This gift of love and right - eous - ness, scorned by the
G D/F♯ Em G/A D D/F♯
3fr
fierc - est drought and storm. What heights of
ones He came to save. 'Til on that
G D/F♯ Asus A D/F♯ G Bm7
love, what depths of peace, when fears are stilled, when striv - ings
cross as Je - sus died, the wrath of God was sat - is -

Asus A G D G A D/F♯
cease. My Com - fort - er, my All in All, here in the
fied, for ev - 'ry sin on Him was laid; here in the
G D/F♯ Em G/A
3fr
1
D G
love of Christ I stand. In Christ a -
death of Christ I
2
D Am7 Em7
live. (Oh.
D Am7
Oh.)

Em7
D
G/D
There in the
D
A/D
G/D
Em/D
ground His bod - y lay, Light of the world by dark - ness
D
G
D
G
A
D/F♯
slain. Then, burst - ing forth in glo - rious day, up from the
G
D/F♯
Em
G/A
3fr
D
G
D/F♯
grave He rose a - gain! And as He stands in vic - to -
cresc.
f

Asus A D/F♯ G Bm7 Asus A G
ry, sin's curse has lost its grip on me. For I am
D G A D/F♯ G D/F♯ Em G/A
3fr
His and He is mine, bought with the pre - cious blood of
D Am7 Em7
Christ. (Oh, oh.)
D G/D D
No guilt in life, no fear in
dim.
mp

A D/F# G D/F# Em A D G
death; this is the pow'r of Christ in me. From life's first
D A D/F# G D/F# Em Asus
cry to fi - nal breath, Je - sus com - mands my des - ti - ny.
cresc.
D D/F# G D/F# Asus A D/F#
No pow'r of hell, no scheme of man, can ev - er
Lead vocal ad lib.
f
G Bm7 Asus A G D G
pluck me from His hand. 'Til He re - turns or calls me

Fmaj7
F6
C
to be born of a vir - gin, dwelt a - mong men.
Fmaj7
F6
Dm
Bdim/D
My ex - am - ple is He. The Word be - came flesh
F
Am
and the light shined a - mong us, His glo - ry re - vealed.
F
C
Liv - ing, He loved me. Dy - ing, He saved
mf

G
Am
Am/G
me. Bur - ied, He car - ried my sins far a - way.
F
C
Ris - ing, He jus - ti - fied free - ly for - ev -
G
C/E
Am
- er. One day He's com - ing; oh, glo - ri - ous day,
F
C
Fmaj7
oh, glo - ri - ous day.

C
Fmaj7
F6
One day they led Him up Cal - va - ry's moun -
One day the grave could con - ceal Him no long -
C
Fmaj7
F6
- tain. One day they nailed Him to die on a tree.
- er. One day the stone rolled a - way from the door.
C
Fmaj7
F6
Suf - fer - ing an - guish, de - spised and re - ject -
Then He a - rose; o - ver death He had con -
C
Fmaj7
F6
- ed, bear - ing our sins, my Re - deem - er is He.
- quered. Now He's as - cend - ed, my Lord ev - er - more.

Dm
Bdim/D
F
The hands that healed na - tions stretched out on a tree
Death could not hold Him, the grave could not keep
Am
G
and took the nails for me.
Him from ris - ing a - gain.
Liv - ing, He loved
cresc.
C
G
me.
Dy - ing, He saved me.
Bur - ied, He car -
f
Am
F
- ried my sins far a - way.
Ris - ing, He jus -

C
G
- ti - fied free - ly for - ev - er. One day He's com -
Am
1
F
C
- ing; oh, glo - ri - ous day, oh, glo - ri - ous day.
Fmaj7
2
F
C
oh, glo ri ous day,
F
C
G
glo - ri - ous day.

F C G Am7
One day the trum - pet will sound for His com - ing.
F C C/E G C/E
One day the skies with His glo - ry will shine.
F C G Am7
Won - der - ful day my Be - loved One bring - ing.
F C
My Sav - ior, Je - sus is mine. Liv - ing, He loved me. Dy - ing, He saved
dim.
mp

G
Am
F
me. Buried, He carried my sins far away.
Rising, He justified freely forever.
C
G
Am
One day He's coming; oh, glorious day,
F
C
F
oh, glorious day,
glorious day,
C
F
oh, glorious day.
f

HOW DEEP THE FATHER'S LOVE FOR US

Words and Music by
STUART TOWNEND

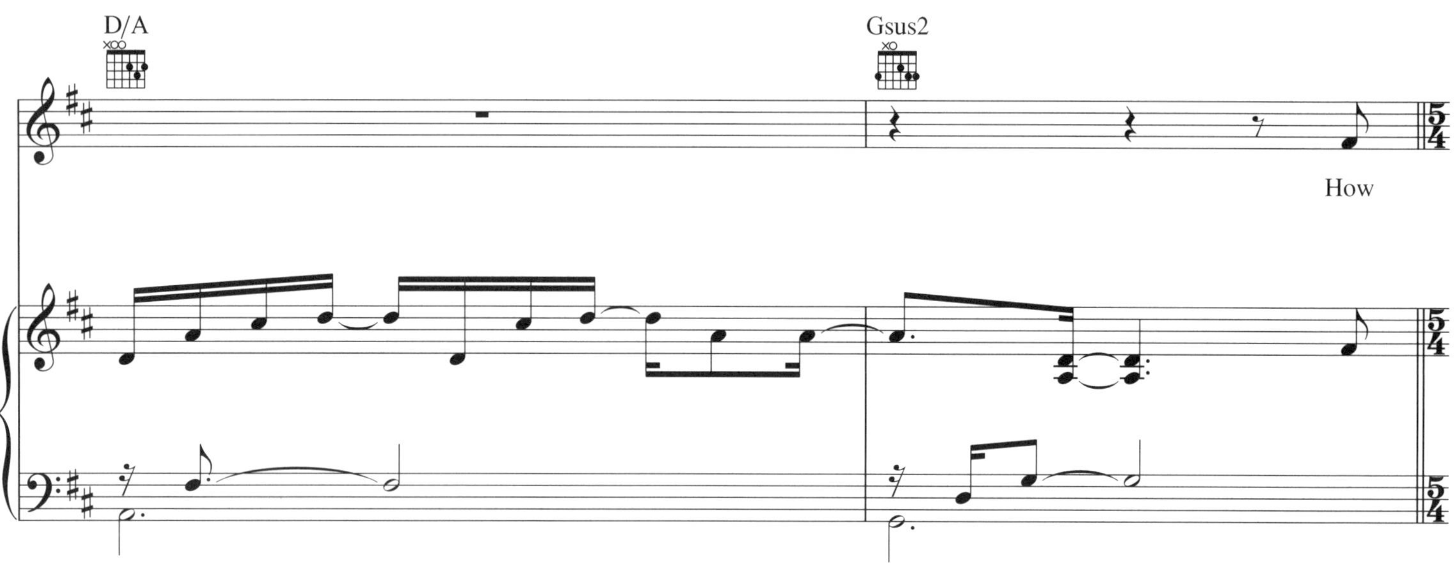

D Em7 D/F♯ G(add9) D/F♯ A D
He should give His on - ly Son to make a wretch His treas - ure. How
shamed, I hear my mock - ing voice call out a - mong the scoff - ers. It
I will boast in Je - sus Christ, His death and res - ur - rec - tion. Why
D Em7 D/F♯ G(add9) D/F♯ Bm7 A
great the pain of sear - ing loss. The Fa - ther turns His face a - way as
was my sin that held Him there un - til it was ac - com - plished. His
should I gain from His re - ward? I can - not give an an - swer, but
D Em7 D/F♯ G(add9) D/F♯ A
wounds which mar the Cho - sen One bring man - y sons to glo -
dy - ing breath has brought me life. I know that it is fin -
this I know with all my heart: His wounds have paid my ran -

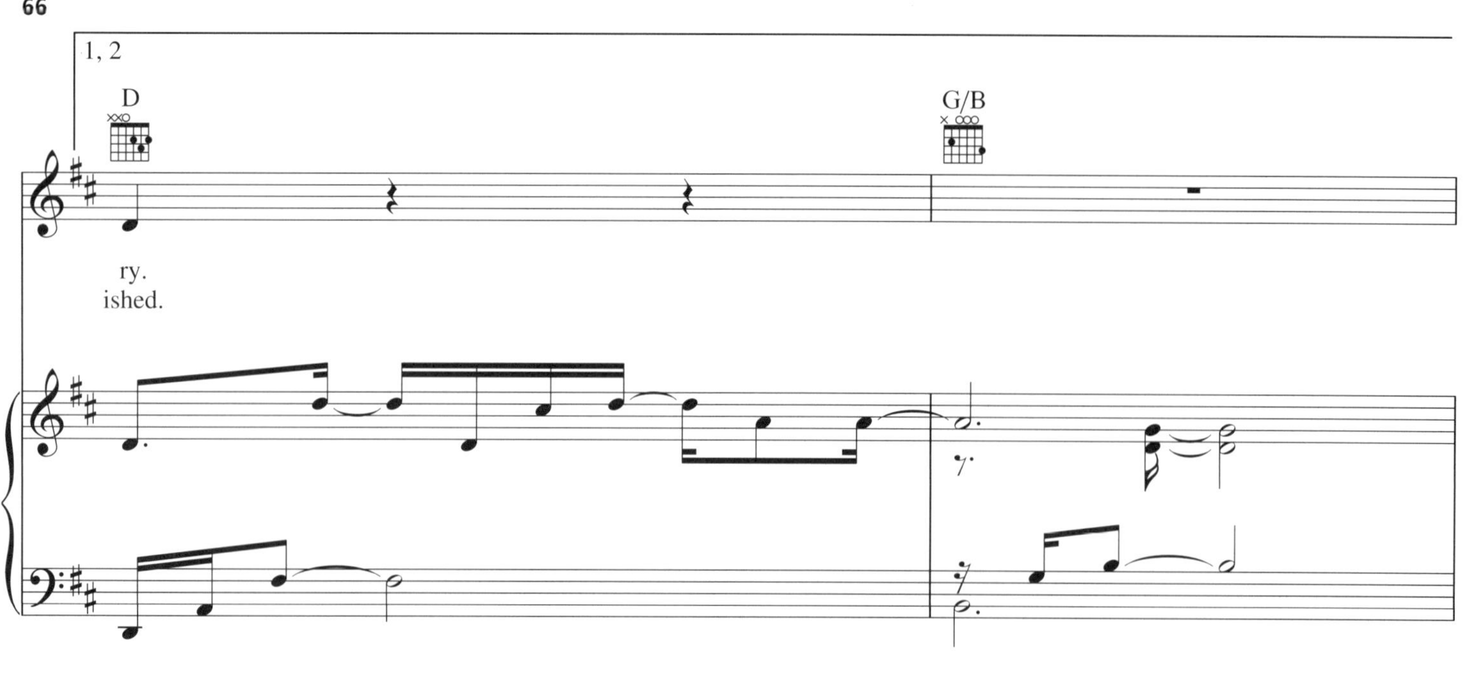
1, 2
D
G/B
ry.
ished.

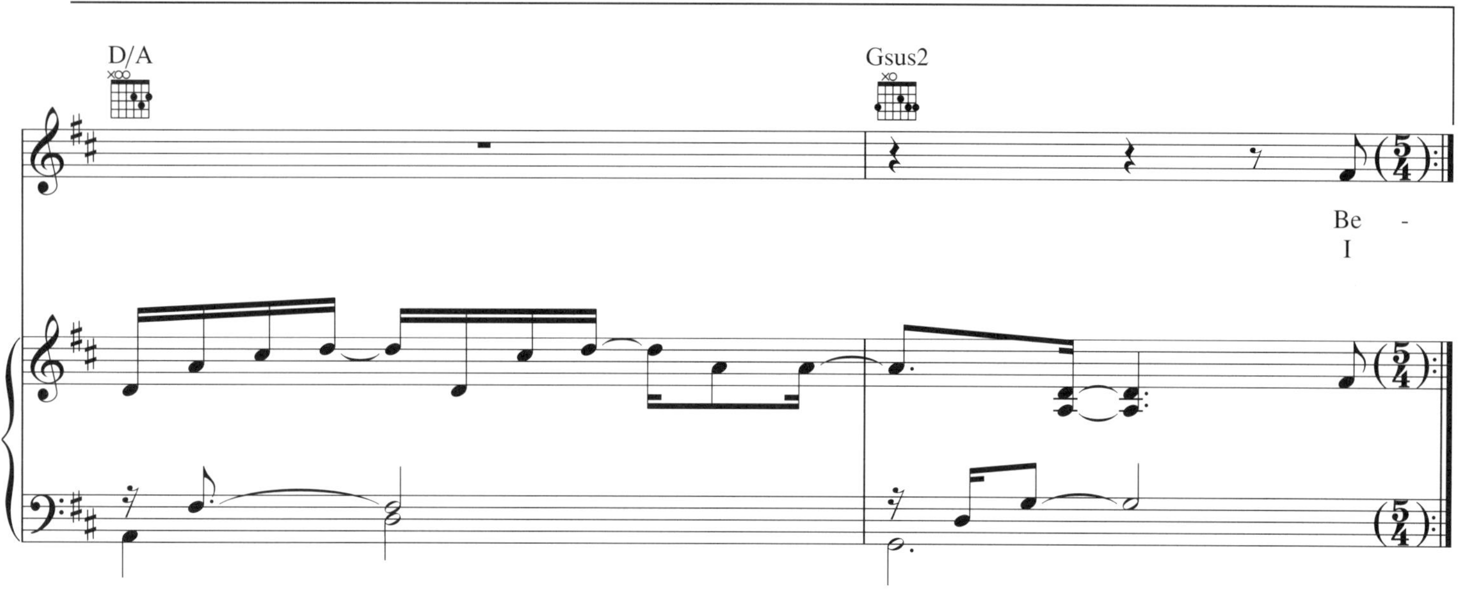
D/A
Gsus2
Be -
I

3
D
Em7
D/F♯
G(add9)
som. Why should I gain from His re - ward? I

D/F♯
Bm7
A
D
Em7
D/F♯
G(add9)
can - not give an an - swer, but this I know with all my heart: His

D/F♯
A
D5
5fr
G/B
wounds have paid my ran - som.

D/A
Gsus2
D
rit.

IT IS WELL

from Walt Disney Pictures' and Walden Media's AMAZING GRACE

Traditional
Arranged by JEREMY CAMP
and ADRIENNE CAMP

D
D/F♯
G
E7sus
ev - er my lot, Thou hast taught me to
nailed to the cross and I'll bear them no
A
G
D/F♯
G
A7
say, "It is well, it is well with my
more. Praise the Lord, praise the Lord, O my
D
Dsus(add2)
5fr
D
soul."
soul
It is well (It is well)
Bm7
F♯m7
D
D/F♯
with my soul. (with my soul.) It is well,

G
C♯dim/E
A
1
D5
5fr
Dsus
it is well with my soul.
f
D
Dsus2
D
2
D
My soul.
We sing,
G
D
"Ho - ly, ho - ly, ho - ly."
We sing, "Ho - ly, ho - ly, ho -
G
- ly." And we sing, "Ho - ly is Your name,
O Most

A
Asus(add2)
A7
G
High."
We sing, "Ho - ly, ho - ly, ho -
D
E7
- ly." We sing, "Ho - ly, ho - ly, ho - ly." And we sing,
G
A
D
Dsus
"Ho - ly is Your name, O Most High."
D
Em7
And Lord, please haste the day when my
mp

G
A
D
Bm
faith shall be sight, the clouds be rolled
Em7
A
Bm/A
A7
A13
5fr
back as a scroll. The
D
Dmaj7/F♯
G
G/F♯
E7sus
E7
trump shall re - sound and the Lord shall de -
mf
Asus
Asus/G
D/F♯
G
A7
scend; E - ven so, it is well with my

D
Dsus
D
soul.
It is well
(It is well)
Bm7
F♯m7
D
D/F♯
with my soul.
(with my soul.)
It is well,
G
C♯dim/E
A
D5
5fr
it is well
with my
soul.
cresc.
It is well
(It is well)
Bm7
with my soul.
f

F♯m7
D
D/F♯
G
(with my soul.)
It is well,
it is well
C♯dim/E
A
Gmaj7
Gm(maj7)
with my soul.
D5
Dsus
D
Dsus2
D
D5
Dsus
D
Dsus2
D
mf

NOTHING BUT THE BLOOD

Words and Music by
MATT REDMAN

* *Recorded a half step lower.*

F
1
C
Am7
G
Je - sus, it's Your blood, Your blood. Your
Je - sus, it's Your blood.
2
C
Am7
G
C
What can wash a - way
our sins?
Am7
What can make us whole a - gain?
G
F
C
Noth - ing but the blood, noth - ing but the blood of Je - sus.

G
F
C
What can wash us pure as snow,
Am7
G
wel - comed as the friends of God?
Noth - ing but Your blood,
F
C
G
F
noth - ing but Your blood, King Je - sus.
C
Am7
C
Am7
Your

C
Am7
cross tes - ti - fies in grace, tells of the Fa - ther's heart
C
Am7
to make a way for us. Now bold - ly we ap - proach,
G
F
not earth - ly con - fi - dence; it's on - ly by Your blood.
C
Am
G
C
What can wash a - way

Am7
our sins?
What can make us whole again?
G
F
C
Noth-ing but the blood,
noth-ing but the blood of Je - sus.
G
F
C
What can wash us pure as snow,
Am7
G
wel-comed as the friends of God?
Noth-ing but Your blood,

F
C
nothing but Your blood, King Jesus.
1
G
F
2
G
F
C
We praise You for the blood.
Am7
Yes, we praise You for the blood.
G
We've been ransomed, we've been held, we've been re-

F
C
G
F
stored and for - giv - en. Thank You, Lord. We
C
Am7
praise You for the blood. We praise You for the blood.
G
What can cleanse the world of sin? Noth - ing but Your blood,
F
C
G
F
C
noth - ing but Your blood, King Je - sus.

JESUS PAID IT ALL

Words and Music by
ALEX NIFONG

* *Recorded a half step lower.*

C
Am7
C
G
Je - sus paid it all,
all to Him I owe.
C
F
C
G
C
C/E
Sin had left a crim-son stain; He washed it white as snow.
f
Fsus2
C/E
Dm7
C/E
Fsus2
C/E
C
C/E
Fsus2
C/E
Dm7
C/E

Fsus2
C/E
C
G
Lord, now in - deed I find Thy pow'r, and Thine a -
when be - fore the throne I stand in Him com -
mf
C
Am7
Fsus2
lone, can change the lep - er's spots and
plete, "Je - sus died, my soul to save," my
To Coda
C
G
C
Am7
melt the heart of stone. Je - sus paid it all,
lips shall still re -
C
G
C
F
all to Him I owe. My sin had left this crim - son stain; He

C
G
C
Fsus2
C/E
washed it white as snow. It's washed a - way, all my
f
Dm7
C/E
Fsus2
C/E
C
sin and all my shame.
Fsus2
C/E
Dm7
C/E
Fsus2
D.S. al Coda
And
CODA
C
peat. Je - sus paid it all, all to Him I
mp

G/C
C
F/C
C
G/C
owe. Sin had left a crim - son stain; He washed it white as
C5
3fr
C
F/C
C
G/C
snow. Sin had left a crim - son stain; He washed it white as
C
G/C
C
snow. He washed it white as snow. He
G/C
C
Csus
3fr
washed it white as snow.
cresc.

C
Oh, praise the One who
paid my debt and raised this life up
1
from the dead. Oh,
2
from the dead. Oh,
C
C/E
Fsus2
C/E
praise the One who paid my debt and
f
ff
Repeat ad lib. and Fade
Optional Ending
Dm7
C/E
Fsus2
C/E
Fsus2
C
raised this life up from the dead. Oh, from the dead.
rit.

JOYFUL, JOYFUL

Words and Music by MARK HALL
and BERNIE HERMS

* Recorded a half step higher.

Gm7
B♭
F
o - p'ning to the sun a - bove.
mf
Csus
3fr
Gm7
B♭sus2
F
Csus
3fr
Gm7
Joy - ful, joy - ful, we a - dore You, God of glo - ry, Lord
B♭sus2
F
Csus
3fr
of love. Hearts un - fold like flow'rs be - fore You,

Gm7
B♭sus2
Gm
3fr
o - p'ning to the sun a - bove.
Melt the clouds of sin
B♭
Gm7
B♭
and sad - ness, drive the dark of doubt a - way.
C
Gm7
Joy - ful, joy - ful we a - dore You.
f
B♭sus2
C
Hearts un - fold like flow'rs be - fore
simile

Gm7
Bbsus2
C
You.
Joy - ful, joy -
Gm7
Bbsus2
- ful, we a - dore You.
Joy - ful, we a - dore
F
Csus
3fr
Gm7
You.
simile
Bbsus2
F
Csus
3fr

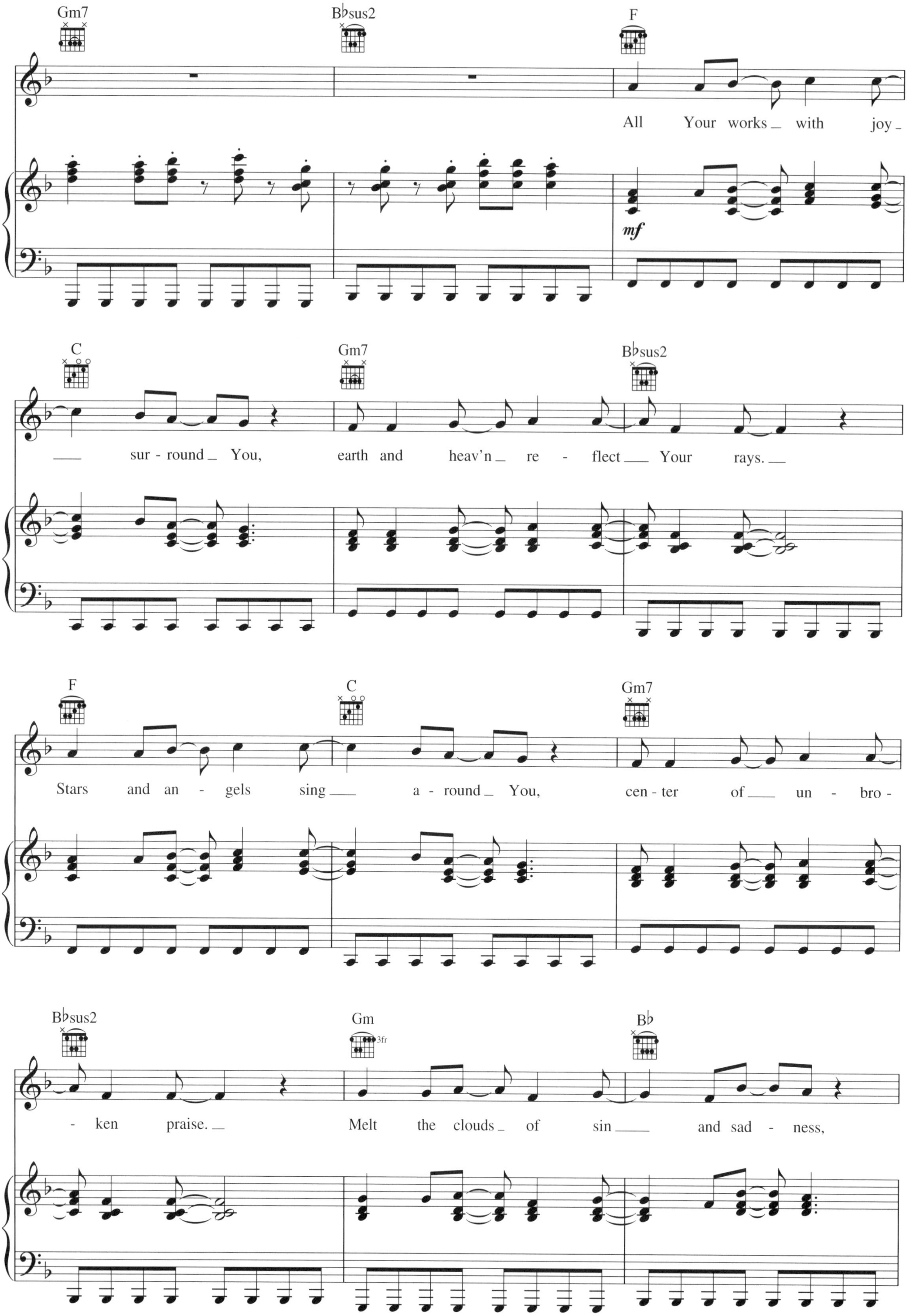

Gm7 Bb♭sus2 F

mf

All Your works with joy

C Gm7 B♭sus2

surround You, earth and heav'n reflect Your rays.

F C Gm7

Stars and angels sing around You, center of unbro-

B♭sus2 Gm B♭

-ken praise. Melt the clouds of sin and sadness,

Gm
3fr
B♭
C
drive the dark of doubt a - way.
Joy - ful, joy -
f
Dm7
B♭
Gm7
B♭
Dm
- ful we a - dore You.
C
Dm7
Gm7
Hearts un - fold like flow'rs be - fore You.
B♭
Dm
C
Dm7
B♭
Joy - ful, joy - ful, we a - dore

Gm7
B♭sus2
Dm
You.
Joy - ful, we a - dore You.
F
C
mp
Gm
C
God, our Fa - ther, Christ, our Broth -
Gm7
B♭maj7
- er, all who live in love are Thine.
Teach us how

C
Gm7
to love each oth - er, lift us to the joy di - vine.
B♭maj7
C
Dm7
B♭
God, our Fa - ther, Christ, our Broth - er, all who live
mf
Gm7
B♭maj7
Dm
in love are Thine. Teach us how
C
Dm7
B♭
Gm7
3fr
to love each oth - er, lift us to the joy di - vine.

1
B♭maj7
Dm
2
B♭maj7
C
God our Fa -
Joy - ful, joy -
- ful, we a - dore You.
f
Dm7
B♭
Gm7
Hearts un - fold like flow'rs be - fore You.
B♭sus2
C
Dm7
B♭
Joy - ful, joy - ful, we a - dore

Gm7
B♭sus2
C
You.
Hearts un - fold
Dm7
B♭
Gm7
B♭
like flow'rs be - fore You.
O God, our Fa -
C
- ther,
all who live,
mf
teach us how to love each oth - er.

JUST AS I AM

from Walt Disney Pictures' and Walden Media's AMAZING GRACE

Traditional
New Verses by NICHOLE NORDEMAN

F/A
B♭
B♭sus2/E♭
B♭/D
F/A
B♭
The bro -
2
B♭/D
E♭sus2
6fr
F
B♭sus
B♭
leave in - stead the stain of grace?
So I
E♭
3fr
Cm
3fr
come in sor - row and I come in shame,
Gm
3fr
I come to the cross with my

Fsus
B♭
pain. Just as I am,
E♭
F
Gm
with - out one plea, but
F/A
E♭/G
F/A
E♭maj7
that Thy blood was shed for me,
B♭/D
E♭
and that Thou bidd'st me come

To Coda
F Gm F/A B♭
to Thee. O Lamb of God,
Cm7 B♭/D E♭maj7
I come, I come.
B♭sus2/E♭ B♭/D F/A B♭ B♭sus2/E♭ B♭/D
F/A B♭ B♭sus2/E♭ B♭/D F/A B♭
The par - don that I found from sin spilled out

B♭sus2/E♭
B♭/D
F/A
B♭
from where the nails went in. My heart will ev - er - more
Gm
E♭
F
3fr
pro - claim: I had not lived un - til that day.
I know
there is a crown for me be - yond where mor - tal eyes can

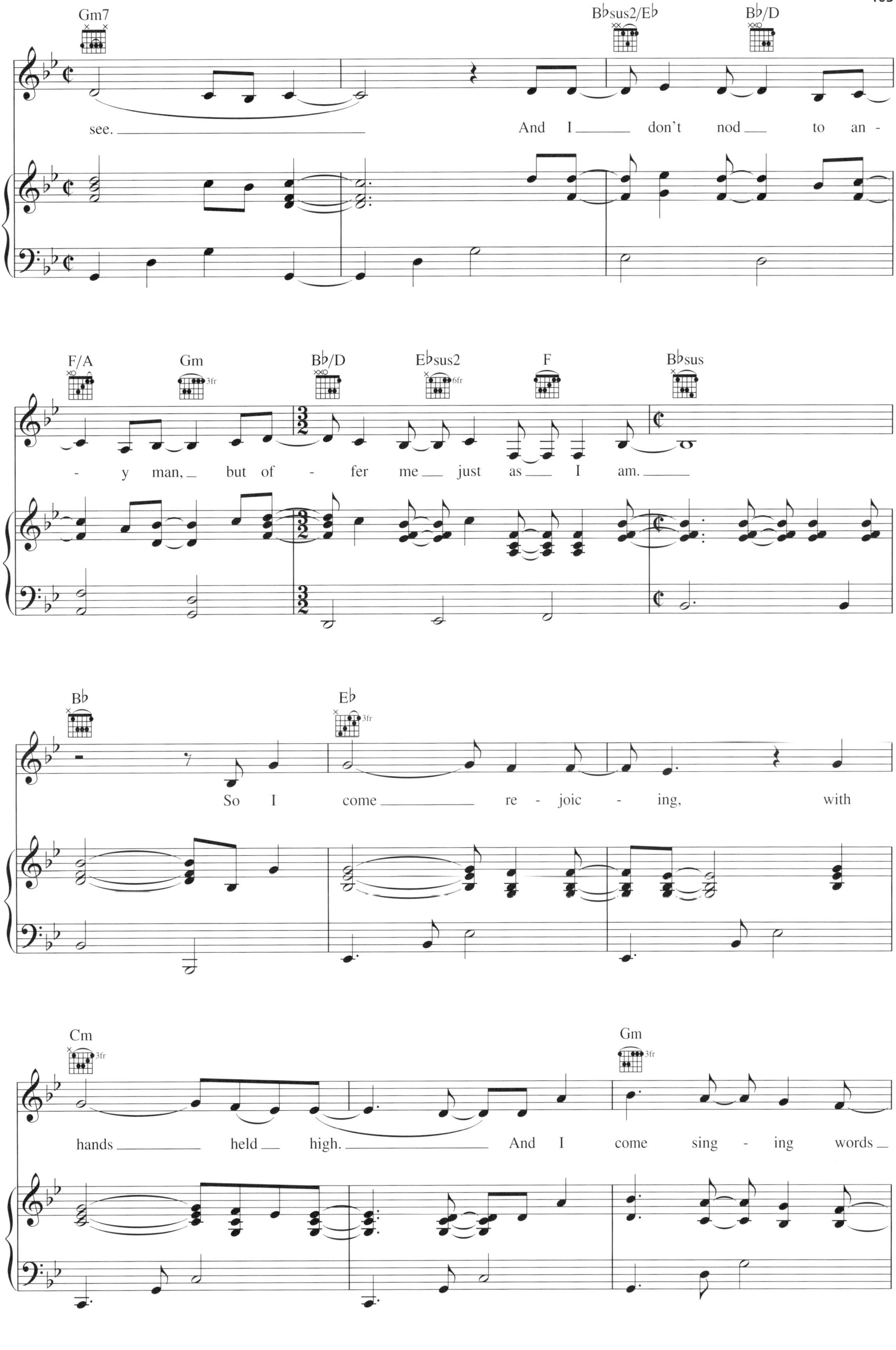

Gm7 B♭sus2/E♭ B♭/D

see. And I don't nod to an-

F/A Gm B♭/D E♭sus2 F B♭sus

-y man, but of-fer me just as I am.

B♭ E♭

So I come re-joic-ing, with

Cm Gm

hands held high. And I come sing-ing words

F
D.S. al Coda
of new life.
Just
CODA
F/A
B♭
Cm7
B♭/D
3fr
of God,
O Lamb
Gm
O Lamb
Gm7
E♭maj9
of God,
I

come,
I
come.
I
come.
O
Lamb
of
God,
I
come.
O
Lamb
of
God,
I
come.

NEW DOXOLOGY

Original Words and Music by *Genevan Psalter* and THOMAS KEN
New Lyrics and Chorus by THOMAS MILLER

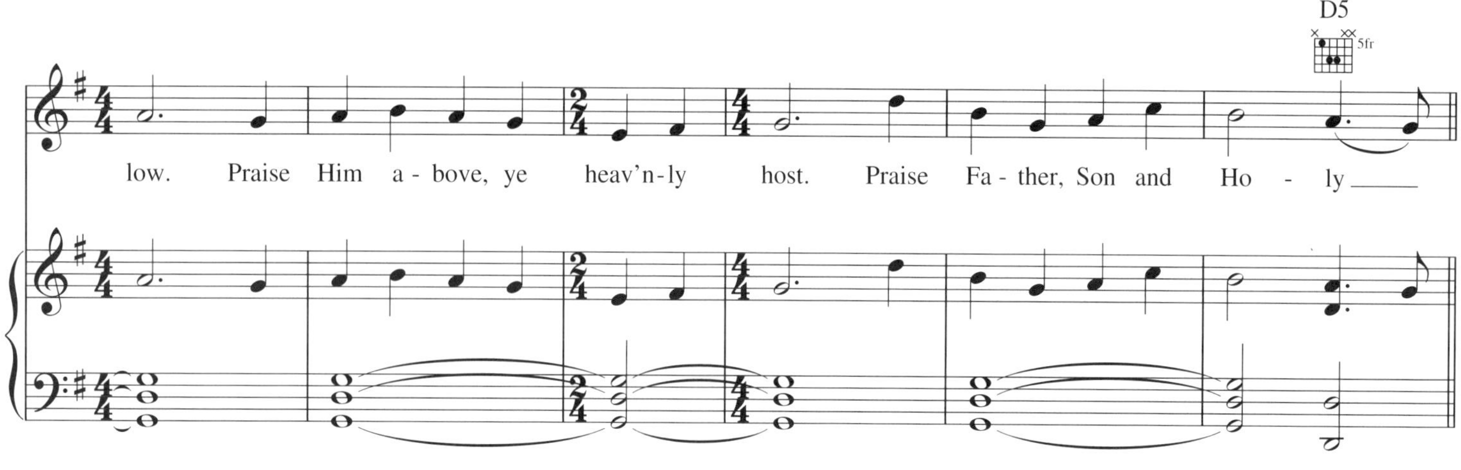

G5
3fr
earth and heav'n - ly saints pro - claim the
to the King; His throne tran - scends. His
D/G
G5
3fr
pow'r and might of His great name. Let
crown and king - dom nev - er ends. Now
us ex - alt on bend - ed knee. Praise
and through - out e - ter - ni - ty, I'll
D
G5
3fr
God, the ho - ly Trin - i - ty.
praise the One who died for me.
cresc.

C
G/B
Praise God, praise God, praise
Am7
Dsus
D
G/B
C
G/B
God, who saved my soul. Praise God, praise God, praise
To Coda
1
Am7
G/D
D
G5
3fr
God, from whom all bless - ings flow.
2
D.S. al Coda
G5
3fr
G/B
Praise flow. Praise

CODA

G5 3fr

flow.

mf

Praise God, from whom all bless - ings flow. Praise

Him, all crea - tures here be - low. Praise Him a - bove, ye

D5 5fr G5 3fr

heav'n - ly host. Praise Fa - ther, Son and Ho - ly Ghost.

O CHURCH ARISE

Words and Music by KEITH GETTY
and STUART TOWNEND

F C F B♭
strength that God has giv - en. With shield of faith and belt of
fight with faith and val - or. When faced with trials on ev - 'ry
Con - quer - or has ris - en. And as the stone lies rolled a -
ser - vant good and faith - ful. As saints of old still line the
C Dm C/E
truth, we'll stand a - gainst the dev - il's lies. An ar - my
side, we know the out - come is se - cure. And Christ will
way, and Christ e - merg - es from the grave, this vic - t'ry
way, re - tell - ing tri - umphs of His grace, we hear their
F C B♭ C
bold whose bat - tle cry is love, reach - ing out to those in dark -
have the prize for which He died, an in - her - i - tance of na -
march con - tin - ues till the day ev - 'ry eye and heart shall see
calls and hun - ger for the day when with Christ we stand in glo -

1, 3
F
ness.
Him.
Our call to
So Spir - it,
2, 4
F
tions.
ry.
Whoa,
C
Gm7
C
F
whoa,
whoa,
whoa.
Whoa,
To Coda
C
Gm7
C
F
D.S. al Coda
whoa,
whoa,
whoa.
Come see the
CODA
Gm7
C
F
hey,
yeah,
whoa.

TAKE MY LIFE

Words and Music by CHRIS TOMLIN
and LOUIE GIGLIO

Asus
D
G/C
Gmaj7/B
- less praise. Take my hands and let them move
from Thee. Take my sil - ver and my gold,
- al throne. Take my love, my Lord, I pour

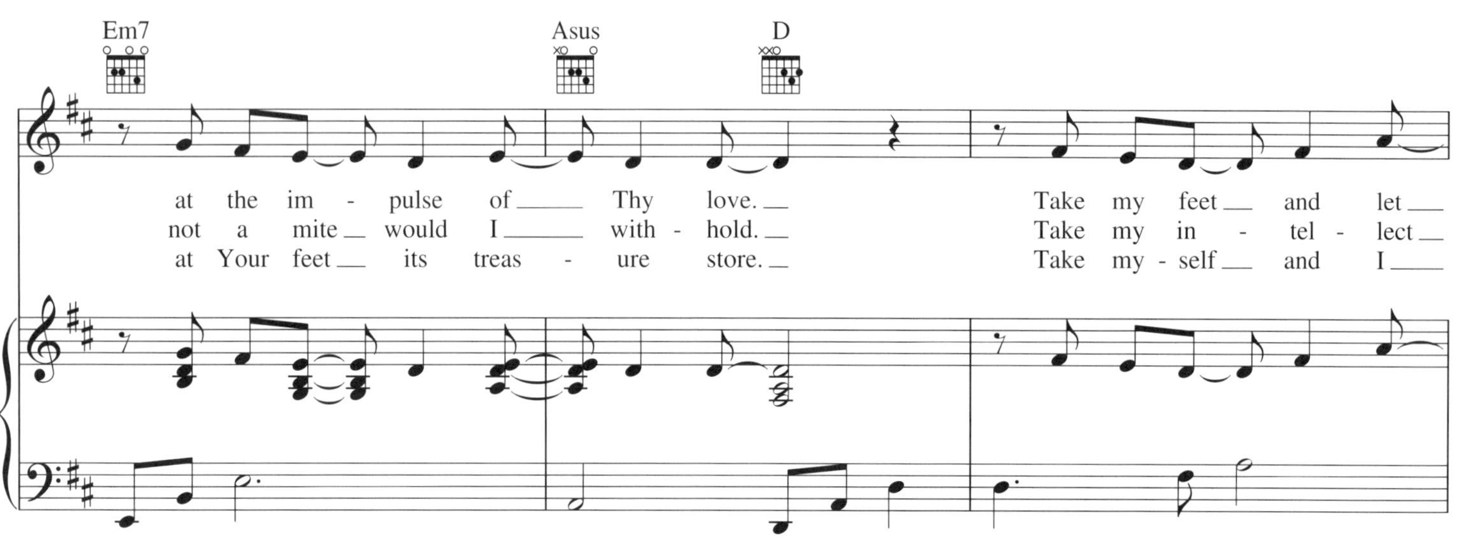
Em7
Asus
D
at the im - pulse of Thy love. Take my feet and let
not a mite would I with - hold. Take my in - tel - lect
at Your feet its treas - ure store. Take my - self and I

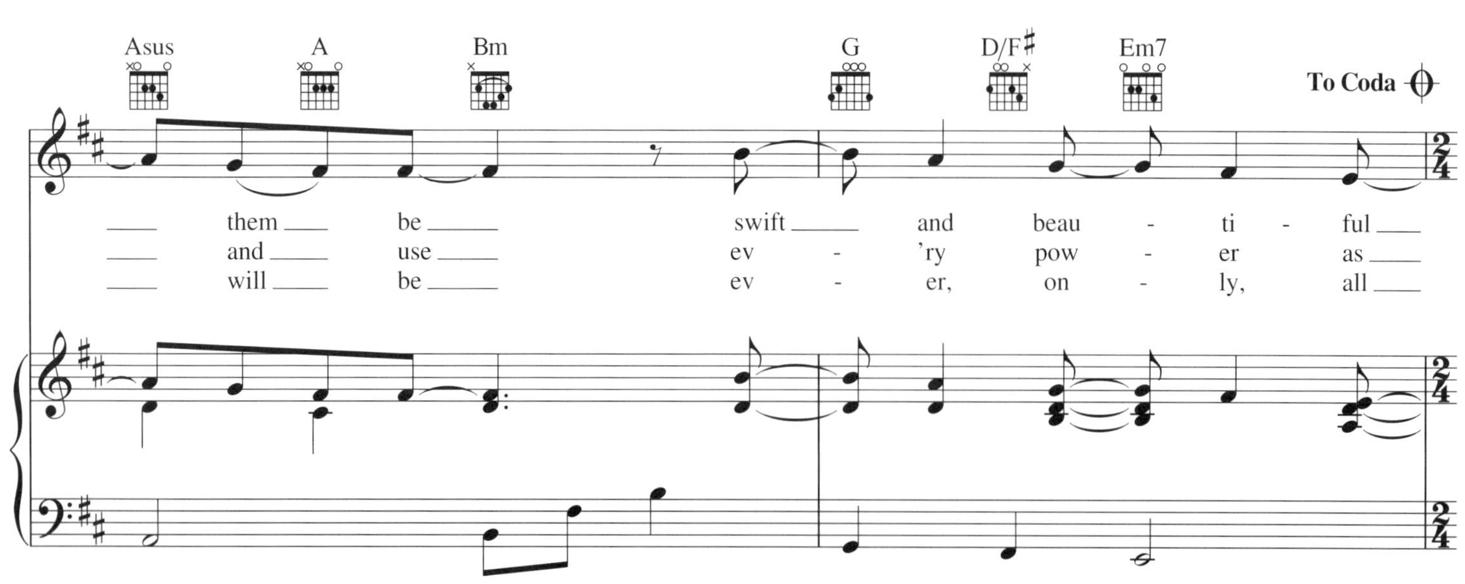
Asus
A
Bm
G
D/F#
Em7
To Coda
them be swift and beau - ti - ful
and use ev - 'ry pow - er as
will be ev - er, on - ly, all

Asus
Dsus2
1
for Thee.
You choose.
2
Em7
Gsus2
Here am I,
all of me.
Asus
Em7
Take my life,
Gsus2
Asus
D.S. al Coda
it's all for Thee.

CODA
Asus
D
A
Bm
for Thee.
Take my - self and I will be ev -
G
D/F♯
Em7
- er, on - ly, all for Thee.
Here am I,
Gsus2
all of me.
mf
Take my life,

Gsus2
Asus
Repeat ad lib.
it's all for Thee.
Here am I,
Final Ending
Asus
Em7
Gsus2
Asus
D
Take my life and let
decresc.
mp
Asus
A
Bm
G
D/F♯
Em7
Asus
D
it be con - se - crat - ed, Lord, to Thee.

O WORSHIP THE KING

Words and Music by
CHRIS TOMLIN

Driving six

A♭5

4fr

A♭

4fr

mp

1

2

f

1

2

O

A♭
D♭/A♭
E♭/A♭
wor - ship the King, all glo - rious a - bove. O
tell of His might, O sing of His grace, whose
meas - ure - less might, in - ef - fa - ble love, while
mf
A♭
D♭
A♭
grate - ful - ly sing His won - der - ful love. Our
robe is the light and can - o - py space. His
an - gels de - light to wor - ship a - bove. Thy
E♭
Shield and De - fend - er, the An - cient of Days, pa -
char - iots of wrath the deep thun - der - clouds form, and
mer - cies how ten - der, how firm to the end, our
A♭
D♭
A♭
vil - ioned in splen - dor and gird - ed with praise.
dark is His path on the wings of the storm.
Mak - er, De - fend - er, Re - deem - er and Friend.
f

1
O
2, 3
D♭
Fm7
You a - lone are the match - less King. To
B♭m7
A♭/C
D♭
You a - lone be all maj - es - ty. Your glo - ries and won - ders, what
Fm7
B♭m7
tongue can re - cite? You breathe in the air,

A♭/C
D♭
To Coda
D.S. al Coda
(take 2nd ending)
You shine in the light. O
CODA
Fm7
You a - lone are the match - less King. To
B♭m7
A♭/C
D♭
You a - lone be all maj - es - ty. Your glo - ries and won - ders, what
Fm7
B♭m7
A♭/C
tongue can re - cite? You breathe in the air, You shine in the light.

Db
Ab/C
Bbm7
Shine in the light, yeah,
Ab/C
Db
yeah. You shine in the light. O
Ab
4fr
wor - ship the King, all glo - rious a - bove. O grate - ful - ly sing His
mp
Eb
3fr
won - der - ful love. Our Shield and De - fend - er, the
mf

A♭
D♭
An - cient of Days, pa - vil - ioned in splen - dor and gird - ed with
A♭
A♭/D♭
A♭
praise.
f
A♭/D♭
A♭
A♭/D♭
A♭
A♭/D♭
A♭

THE POWER OF THE CROSS
(Oh to See the Dawn)

Words and Music by KEITH GETTY
and STUART TOWNEND

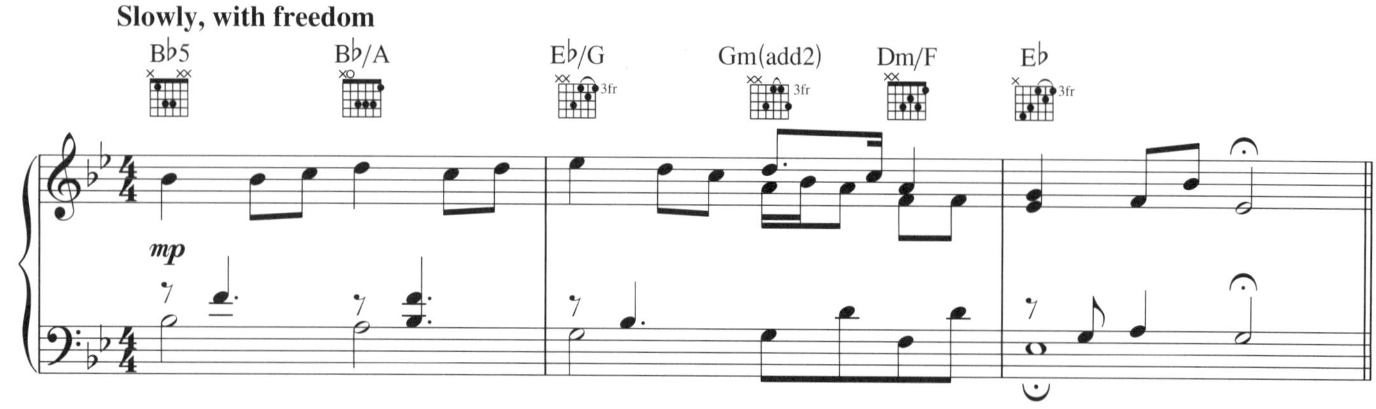

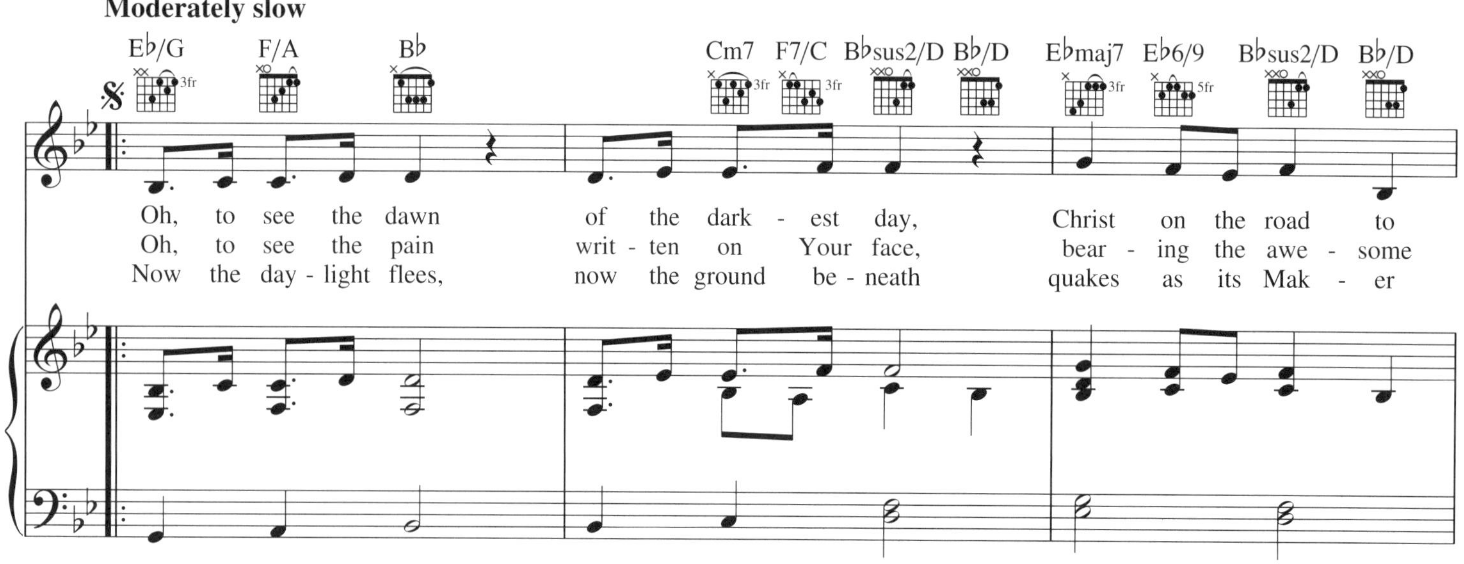

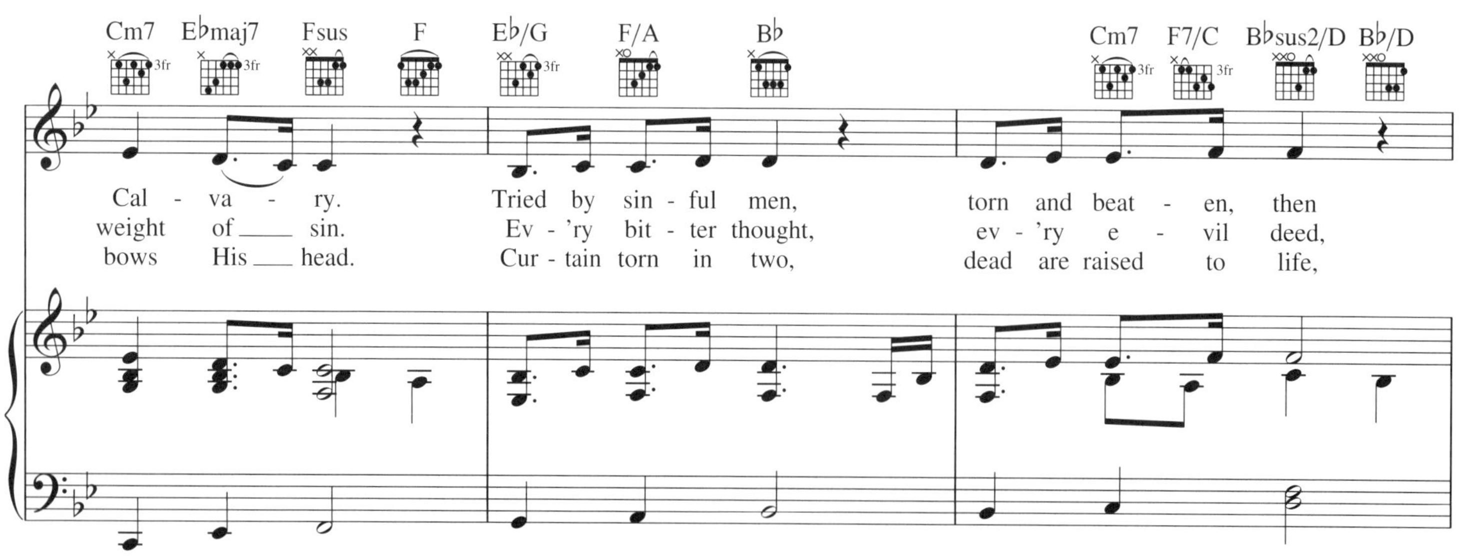

E♭maj7 E♭6/9 B♭sus2/D E♭maj7 Fsus F B♭sus2/D E♭ F/A
nailed to a cross of wood.
crown - ing Your blood - stained brow. This, the pow'r of the
"Fin - ished!" the vic - t'ry cry.
B♭ B♭/D E♭ F/A B♭ B♭/D E♭ C/E
cross: Christ be - came sin for us. Took the blame, bore the
F F/E♭ B♭/D E♭
To Coda
1
Fsus F B♭ E♭maj7 E♭6
wrath. We stand for - giv - en at the cross.
B♭/F Fsus F
2
Fsus F B♭ Gm11 Gm
at the cross.

E♭maj7
F
Fsus
F
E♭/G
F/A
D.S. al Coda
CODA
F
B♭
E♭/G
F/A
B♭
G/B
C/E
F/A
Gsus
G
at the cross.
F/A
G/B
C
Dm7
C/E
F
C/E
Oh, to see my name writ - ten in the wounds, for through Your suf - f'ring
Dm7
C/F
Gsus
G
F/A
G/B
C
Dm7
C/E
I am free. Death is crushed to death, life is mine to live,

F C/E Gsus G C/E F G/B
won through Your self - less love. This, the pow'r of the
C C/E F G/B C C/E
cross: Son of God slain for us. What a
F D/F♯ G G/F C/E F Gsus G
love, what a cost. We stand for-giv - en at the
C F/C C F/C C
cross.
3fr

THE SOLID ROCK
(On Christ the Solid Rock)

Traditional
Arranged by CHARLIE HALL, TRENT AUSTIN
and KENDALL COMBES

Bsus
E
Bsus
right - eous - ness. I dare not trust the sweet - est frame, but
chang - ing grace. In ev - 'ry high and storm - y gale, my
whelm - ing flood. When all a - round my soul gives way, He
A
Bsus
E
whol - ly lean on Je - sus' name.
an - chor holds with - in the veil.
then is all my hope and stay.
A
On Christ, the sol - id Rock, I stand. All
E
Bsus
E
oth - er ground is sink - ing sand, all oth - er ground is

Bsus
E
Esus2
E/G♯
Asus2
sink - ing sand.
Esus2
1, 2
E/G♯
Asus2
3
E/G♯
Asus2
When
His
Esus2
E/G♯
Asus2
E5
When He shall come with
trum - pet sound, O may I then in Him be found dressed

Bsus
A
in His right - eous - ness a - lone, fault - less to stand be -
Bsus
E
A
Bsus
E
fore the throne, fault - less to stand be - fore the throne, fault -
A
E5
Esus2
less to stand be - fore the throne.
E/G♯
Asus2
Esus2
E/G♯
Asus2

Esus2
E/G♯
Asus2
You are our Rock.
Vocal ad lib. on repeat

Esus2
E/G♯
Asus2
Esus2
You are our Rock.

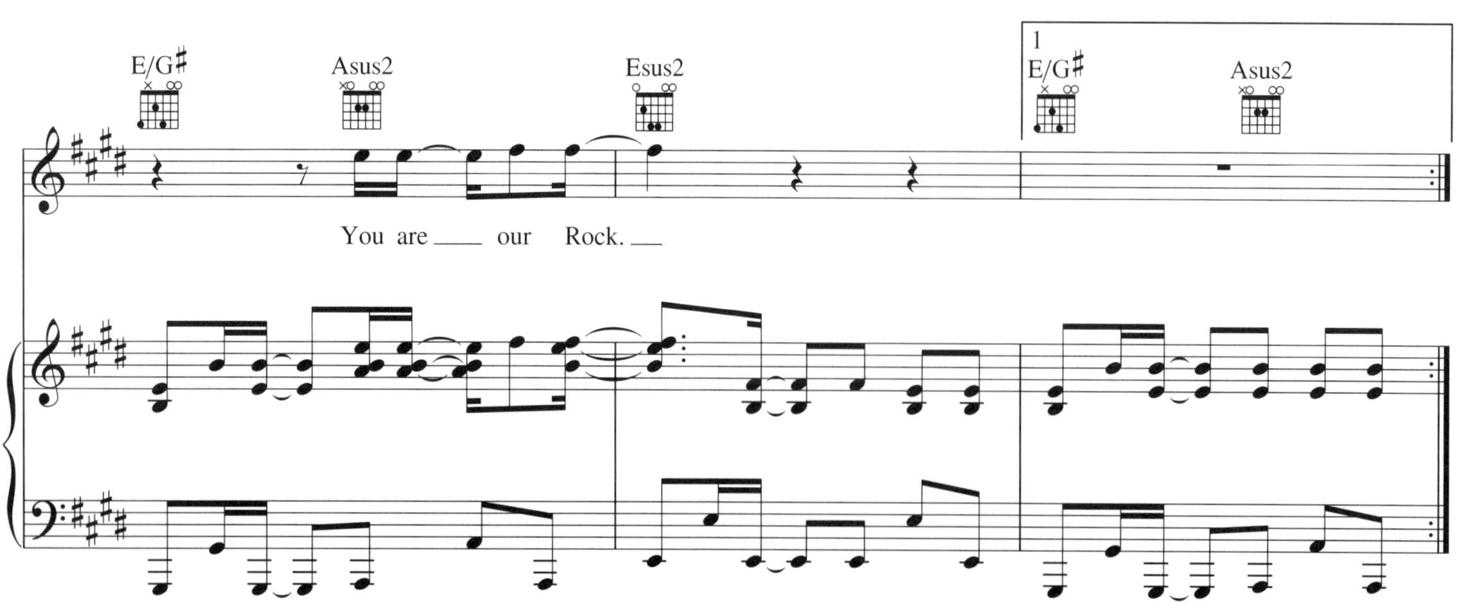

E/G♯
Asus2
Esus2
1
E/G♯
Asus2
You are our Rock.

2
E/G♯
Asus2
Esus2
E/G♯
Asus2
On

E5
Christ, the sol - id Rock, I stand. All oth - er ground is

sink - ing sand, all oth - er ground is sink - ing sand.

SPEAK O LORD

Words and Music by STUART TOWNEND
and KEITH GETTY

E♭ E♭/D♭ A♭/C D♭maj7 A♭/C E♭ E♭/D♭ A♭/C
light of Christ might be seen to-day in our acts of love and our
D♭maj7 E♭sus E♭ D♭/F E♭/G A♭ D♭ A♭/C
deeds of faith. Speak, O Lord, and ful-fill in us all Your
D♭ A♭/C D♭ E♭sus E♭ A♭ D♭
pur-pos-es for Your glo-ry.
A♭/C E♭sus E♭ D♭/F E♭/G A♭ D♭ A♭/C
Teach us, Lord, full o-be-di-ence, ho-ly
Speak, O Lord, and re-new our minds. Help us
3fr
6fr
4fr

Db Ab/C Fm7 Eb/G Db/F Eb/G Ab
3fr 3fr 4fr
rev - er - ence, true hu - mil - i - ty. Test our thoughts and our
grasp the heights of Your plans for us. Truths un - changed from the
Db Ab/C Db Ab/C Db
at - ti - tudes in the ra - di - ance of Your
dawn of time that will ech - o down through e -
Ebsus Eb Ab Eb Eb/Db Ab/C
6fr 3fr 4fr 3fr
pu - ri - ty. Cause our faith to rise, cause our
ter - ni - ty. And by grace we'll stand on Your
Dbmaj7 Ab/C Eb Eb/Db Ab/C
3fr
eyes to see Your ma - jes - tic love and au -
prom - is - es, and by faith we'll walk as You

D♭maj7
E♭sus
E♭
D♭/F
E♭/G
A♭
D♭
A♭/C
thor - i - ty. Words of pow'r that can nev - er fail, let the
walk with us. Speak, O Lord, 'til Your church is built and the
D♭
A♭/C
D♭
1
E♭sus
E♭
A♭
D♭
truth pre - vail o - ver un - be - lief.
earth is filled with Your
A♭/C
E♭sus
E♭
2
E♭sus
E♭
A♭
D♭
glo - ry.
A♭/C
A♭
A♭/C
D♭
E♭sus
E♭
A♭sus
A♭
rit.

THERE IS A HIGHER THRONE

Words and Music by KEITH GETTY
and KRISTYN LENNOX GETTY

E A B
Be - fore the Son we'll stand, made fault - less
He'll wipe each tear - stained eye as thirst and
Esus E B/D♯ B/C♯ C♯m B B/A A
4fr
through the Lamb. Be - liev - ing _ hearts find prom - ised grace,
hun - ger die. The Lamb be - comes our Shep - herd King;
F♯m7(add4) Bsus B Bsus2 B E/G♯
sal - va - tion _ comes. Hear heav - en's
we'll reign with _ Him.
A B Esus E B/D♯
voic - es _ sing, their thun - d'rous an - them _ rings. Through

B/C♯
C♯m
4fr
B/A
A
F♯m7(add4)
em - 'rald courts and sap - phire skies their prais - es
Bsus
B
Bsus2
B
E/G♯
A
rise. All glo - ry, wis - dom, pow'r,
B
Esus
E
B/D♯
4fr
B/C♯
C♯m/B
strength, thanks and hon - or are to God our King, who
B/A
A
F♯m7(add4)
Bsus
B
To Coda
1
E
B/E
reigns on high for - ev - er - more.

E/A
B/A
E
B/E
E/A
B/A
2
F♯m7
more.
G♯m7
4fr
Amaj9
Bsus
B
D.S. al Coda
For - ev - er - more.
CODA
E
B/E
E/A
B/A
more.
(Vocal 1st time only)
E
B/E
E/A
B/A
Play 3 times
E

THE WONDERFUL CROSS

Words and Music by JESSE REEVES,
CHRIS TOMLIN and J.D. WALT

loss, and pour con - tempt on
meet, or thorns com - pose so
vine, de - mands my soul, my
all my pride.
rich a crown?
life, my all.
1
2, 3
O the
G
D/F♯
won - der - ful cross, O the won - der - ful cross
bids me come and die and find that I may tru -

A
G
-ly live.
O the won-der-ful cross,
D/F♯
G
D/F♯
O the won-der-ful cross;
all who gath-
G
D/F♯
A
To Coda
-er here by grace draw near and bless Your name.
D.S. al Coda
(take 2nd ending)
CODA
D